come! These stories have had a long journey into print. Here's a brief history of the book you hold in your hands:

on my arrival in the Arctic in 1984, there were grandiose plans to write the great Canadian novel. Instead, I did a variety of all commercial art jobs, helped found and chaired the local library board, and created several educational comics for federal territorial agencies. A planned 1986 World Exposition, in Vancouver, offered another opportunity: the NWT pavilion needed hentic northern products to sell. I proposed a comic book with stories of the arctic past, present, and future which I would write d draw. My proposal was accepted. Expo 86 was a smash success. The NWT pavilion was ranked in the top ten, with huge atten-ce numbers, and the first Arctic Comics sold very well.

well, I was asked to produce a similar book for the Canadian Pavilion at the 1992 World Exposition in Seville, Spain. It was risioned as a cross between a 'European-style' comics album and North American comics with a variety of stories by Inuit writ-and artists --creators with a closer, clearer cultural connection to Inuit stories and the Arctic. Michael Kusugak was just begin-g his distinguished writing career and offered a touching poem I thought could be adapted into a comics story. Susan Thurston rley did a beautiful job with it. Michael's younger brother Jose wanted to tell one of the many legendary stories of Kiviuq, who he cribed as an Arctic Ulysses. I was particularly pleased when the wonderful Inuit artist Germaine Arnaktauyok agreed to illus-e this tale. A dramatic story about possible future energy options for the north seemed like a good idea, and my old friend and ntor George Freeman brought my writing to life. "The Great Softball Massacre", an amusing story of the Arctic present (circa 0) was a sequel to "My Northern Summer Vacation" from the Expo 86 comic.

reasons I won't detail here, the window for having the book ready for Expo 92 was missed. Fast forward to a few years ago. end and fellow comics creator Lovern Kindzierski urges me to blow the dust off Arctic Comics 92. He introduces me to Alexan-Finbow at Renegade Entertainment Arts. Alexander is interested. The book holds up. It's still a rare combination of indigenous nics stories written and drawn by Inuit and other northerners --people who live, or have lived, in the Arctic. A world bursting h the magic of discovery, drama, humour, and beauty.

heartfelt thanks goes out to all the writers and artists involved for being so patient. Sadly, some who contributed to, or ported this book did not live to see its publication. **Jose Kusugak (1950-2011)** was intelligent, creative, a born raconteur. His tural and political contribution to the people of the north was immense. He helped standardize the syllabic writing system Inuktitut, was the CBC Kivalliq's area manager for over a decade, and negotiated the creation of Nunavut. He understood the portance of storytelling. **Lisa Lugtig (1957-2003)** dreamt of living and working in the north since age 12. She became a doctor, moved to Rankin Inlet, and grew together. Without her, this book would never have existed. Lovern Kindzierski is very much e! Not only did he do the colour separations on most of these stories, he reminded me about this book long after I'd put it aside lo other work. I am sure there are many others I should thank, but time and age has effaced them from my increasingly poor mory.

holas Burns, March 2016

iuq vs Big Bee: written by Jose Kusugak art by Germaine Arnaktauyok
Waiting: written by Michael Kusugak art by Susan Thurston Shirley
e Great Slo-Pitch Massacre, Film Nord and **Sheldon the Sled Dog** by Nicholas Burns
zzard House: written by Nicholas Burns art by George Freeman
blisher Alexander Finbow-Edited by Nicholas Burns-Colour by Lovern Kindzierski & Laurie E. Smith-Production by an Senka

Published by Renegade Arts Canmore Ltd trading as Renegade Arts Entertainment Ltd.
ic Comics ISBN: 9781987825039 Arctic Comics, the story, characters, world and designs are copyright their respective writers and artists s publication is copyright Renegade Arts Canmore Ltd 2016

Renegade Arts Entertainment is Alexander Finbow Doug Bradley Alan Grant John Finbow Luisa Harkins Jennifer Taylor.
il: contact@renegademail.com twitter: @RenegadeArtsEnt
ck out more titles from Renegade Arts Entertainment at our website egadeartsentertainment.com
ted in Canada. Published with financial support from the Government of Alberta ugh the Publishing Organization Operating Grant.

ENVIRONMENTAL BENEFITS STATEMENT

Renegade Arts Canmore Ltd saved the following resources by printing the pages of this book on chlorine free paper made with 10% post-consumer waste.

TREES	WATER	SOLID WASTE	GREENHOUSE GASES
1	386	26	71
FULLY GROWN	GALLONS	POUNDS	POUNDS

Environmental impact estimates were made using the Environmental Paper Network Paper Calculator 3.2. For more information visit www.papercalculator.org.

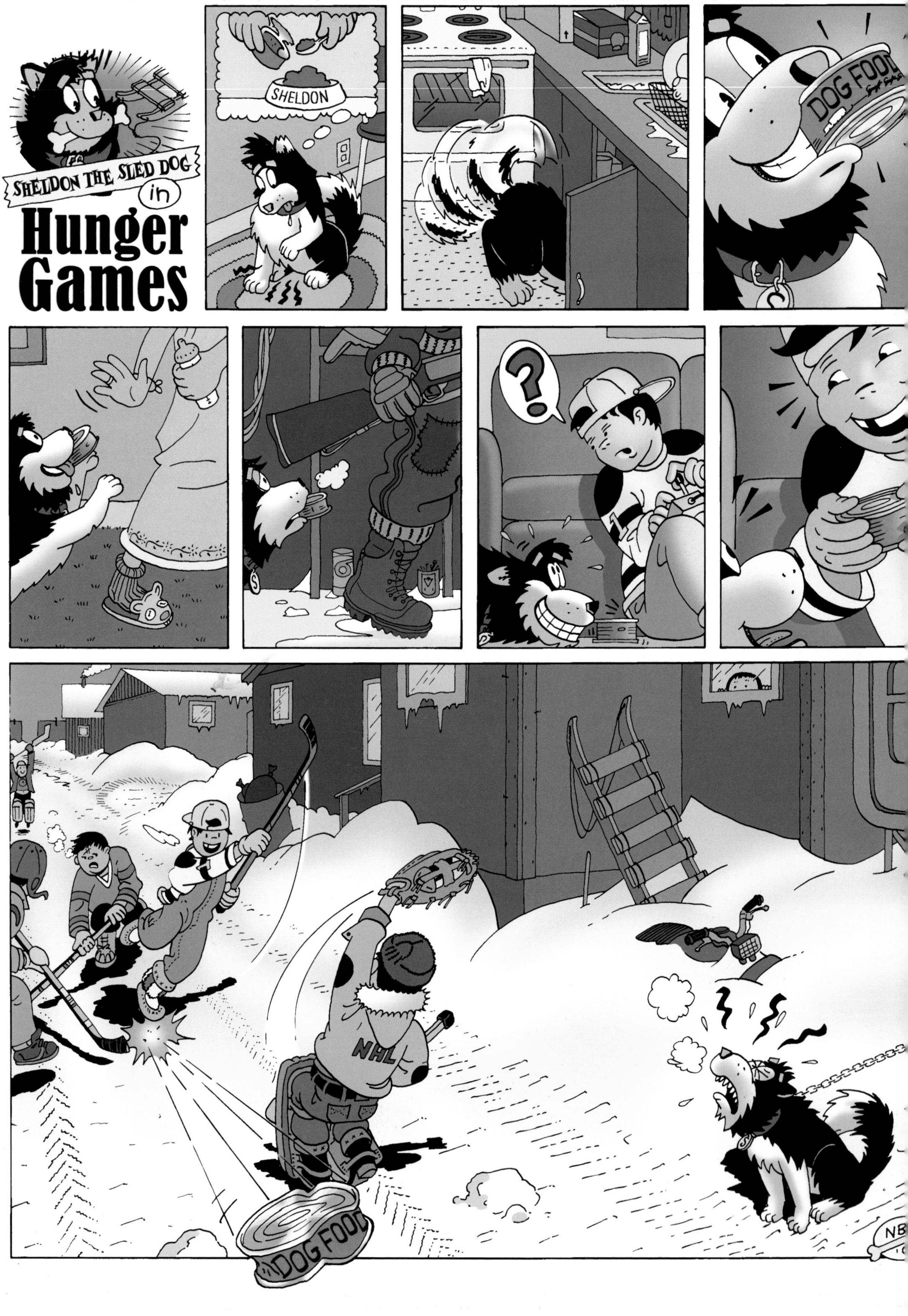
SHELDON THE SLED DOG
in
Hunger Games
SHELDON
DOG FOOD
?
NHL
DOG FOOD
NB

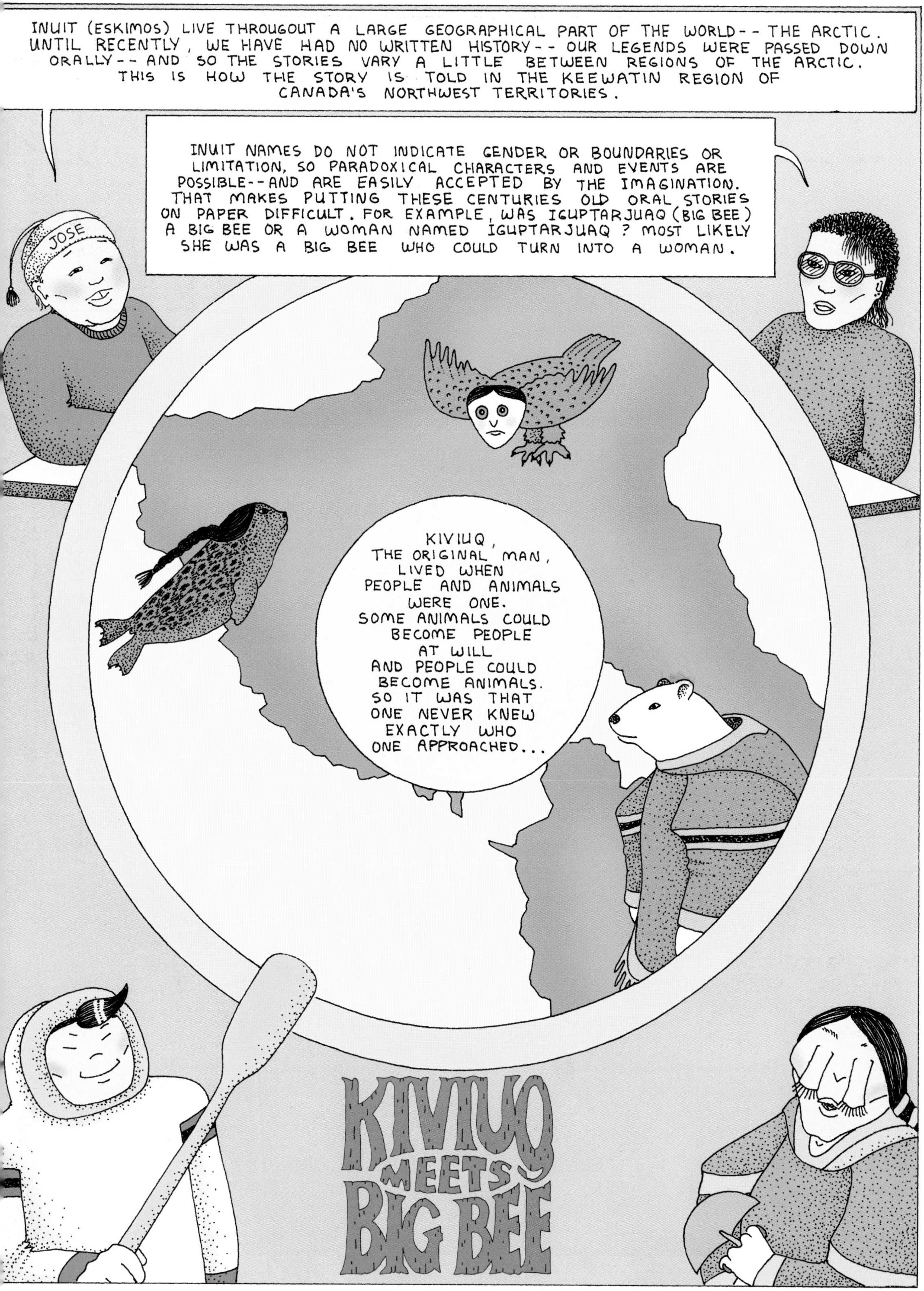
INUIT (ESKIMOS) LIVE THROUGOUT A LARGE GEOGRAPHICAL PART OF THE WORLD-- THE ARCTIC. UNTIL RECENTLY, WE HAVE HAD NO WRITTEN HISTORY-- OUR LEGENDS WERE PASSED DOWN ORALLY-- AND SO THE STORIES VARY A LITTLE BETWEEN REGIONS OF THE ARCTIC. THIS IS HOW THE STORY IS TOLD IN THE KEEWATIN REGION OF CANADA'S NORTHWEST TERRITORIES.
INUIT NAMES DO NOT INDICATE GENDER OR BOUNDARIES OR LIMITATION, SO PARADOXICAL CHARACTERS AND EVENTS ARE POSSIBLE--AND ARE EASILY ACCEPTED BY THE IMAGINATION. THAT MAKES PUTTING THESE CENTURIES OLD ORAL STORIES ON PAPER DIFFICULT. FOR EXAMPLE, WAS IGUPTARJUAQ (BIG BEE) A BIG BEE OR A WOMAN NAMED IGUPTARJUAQ? MOST LIKELY SHE WAS A BIG BEE WHO COULD TURN INTO A WOMAN.
JOSE
KIVIUQ, THE ORIGINAL MAN, LIVED WHEN PEOPLE AND ANIMALS WERE ONE. SOME ANIMALS COULD BECOME PEOPLE AT WILL AND PEOPLE COULD BECOME ANIMALS. SO IT WAS THAT ONE NEVER KNEW EXACTLY WHO ONE APPROACHED...
KIVIUQ MEETS BIG BEE

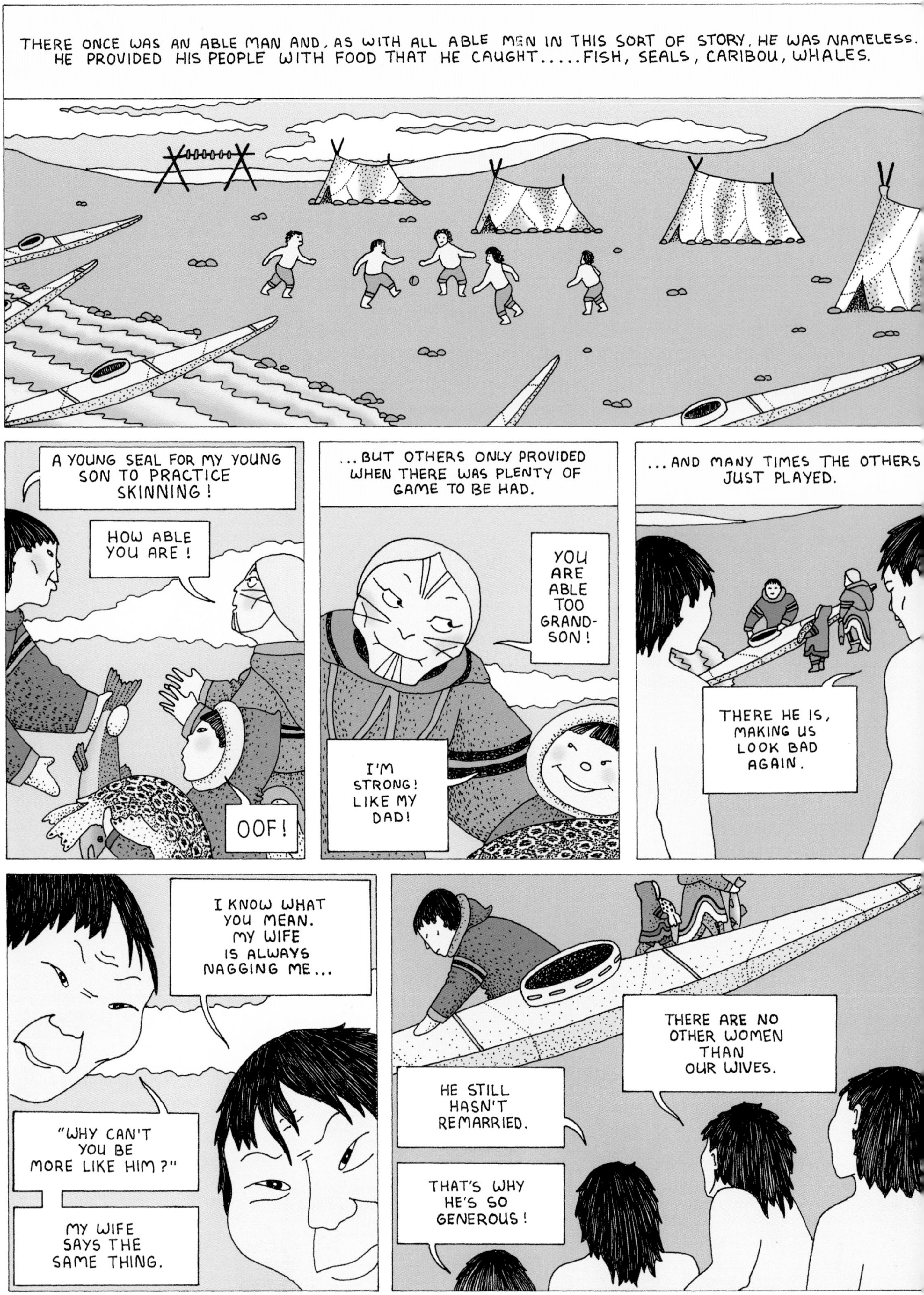
THERE ONCE WAS AN ABLE MAN AND, AS WITH ALL ABLE MEN IN THIS SORT OF STORY, HE WAS NAMELESS. HE PROVIDED HIS PEOPLE WITH FOOD THAT HE CAUGHT.....FISH, SEALS, CARIBOU, WHALES.
A YOUNG SEAL FOR MY YOUNG SON TO PRACTICE SKINNING!
HOW ABLE YOU ARE!
OOF!
...BUT OTHERS ONLY PROVIDED WHEN THERE WAS PLENTY OF GAME TO BE HAD.
YOU ARE ABLE TOO GRANDSON!
I'M STRONG! LIKE MY DAD!
...AND MANY TIMES THE OTHERS JUST PLAYED.
THERE HE IS, MAKING US LOOK BAD AGAIN.
I KNOW WHAT YOU MEAN. MY WIFE IS ALWAYS NAGGING ME...
"WHY CAN'T YOU BE MORE LIKE HIM?"
MY WIFE SAYS THE SAME THING.
HE STILL HASN'T REMARRIED.
THERE ARE NO OTHER WOMEN THAN OUR WIVES.
THAT'S WHY HE'S SO GENEROUS!

MY DAD IS THE BEST HUNTER IN THE CAMP!

QUIETLY, GRANDCHILD QUIETLY...

...JEALOUS EARS ARE EVERYWHERE.

I CAN TASTE THAT SEAL ALREADY!

WHERE IS YOUR FATHER?

I DON'T KNOW.

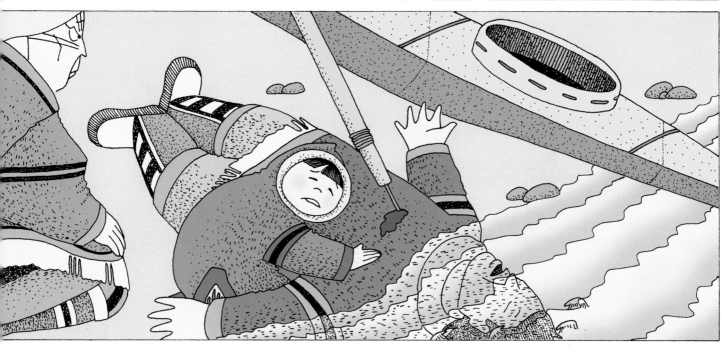

THERE WAS NO TIME FOR MOURNING IN THOSE DAYS.

THINGS WENT BACK TO "NORMAL".

FATHER! FATHER!

COME, GRANDCHILD.

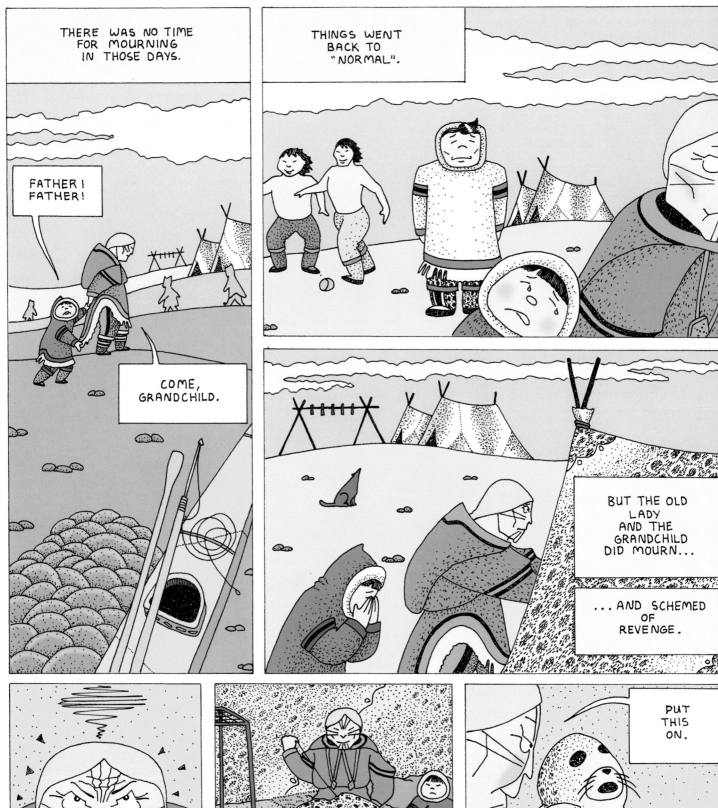

BUT THE OLD LADY AND THE GRANDCHILD DID MOURN...

...AND SCHEMED OF REVENGE.

GRANDCHILD, BRING ME THAT YOUNG SEAL'S SKIN.

THE OLD LADY WAS AN ANGAKKUQ...A SHAMAN. SHE PLANNED TO GET RID OF ALL THE MEN SHE THOUGHT HAD A PART IN THE KILLING OF HER SON.

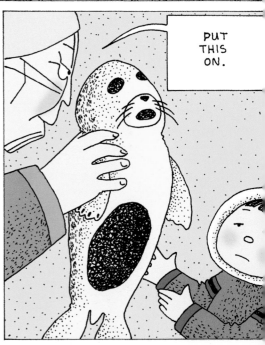

PUT THIS ON.

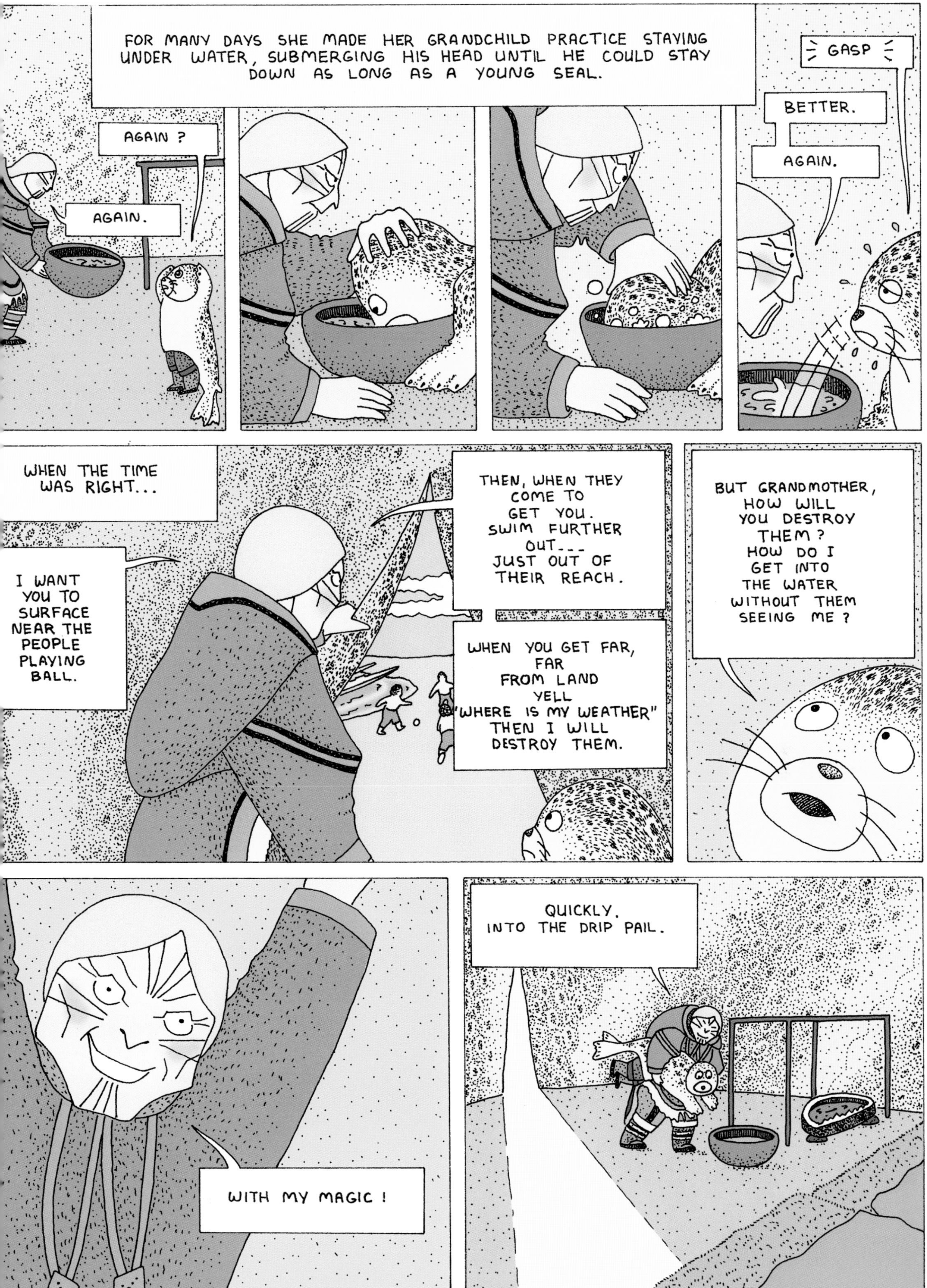
FOR MANY DAYS SHE MADE HER GRANDCHILD PRACTICE STAYING UNDER WATER, SUBMERGING HIS HEAD UNTIL HE COULD STAY DOWN AS LONG AS A YOUNG SEAL.
AGAIN?
AGAIN.
GASP
BETTER.
AGAIN.
WHEN THE TIME WAS RIGHT...
I WANT YOU TO SURFACE NEAR THE PEOPLE PLAYING BALL.
THEN, WHEN THEY COME TO GET YOU. SWIM FURTHER OUT--- JUST OUT OF THEIR REACH.
WHEN YOU GET FAR, FAR FROM LAND YELL "WHERE IS MY WEATHER" THEN I WILL DESTROY THEM.
BUT GRANDMOTHER, HOW WILL YOU DESTROY THEM? HOW DO I GET INTO THE WATER WITHOUT THEM SEEING ME?
WITH MY MAGIC!
QUICKLY. INTO THE DRIP PAIL.

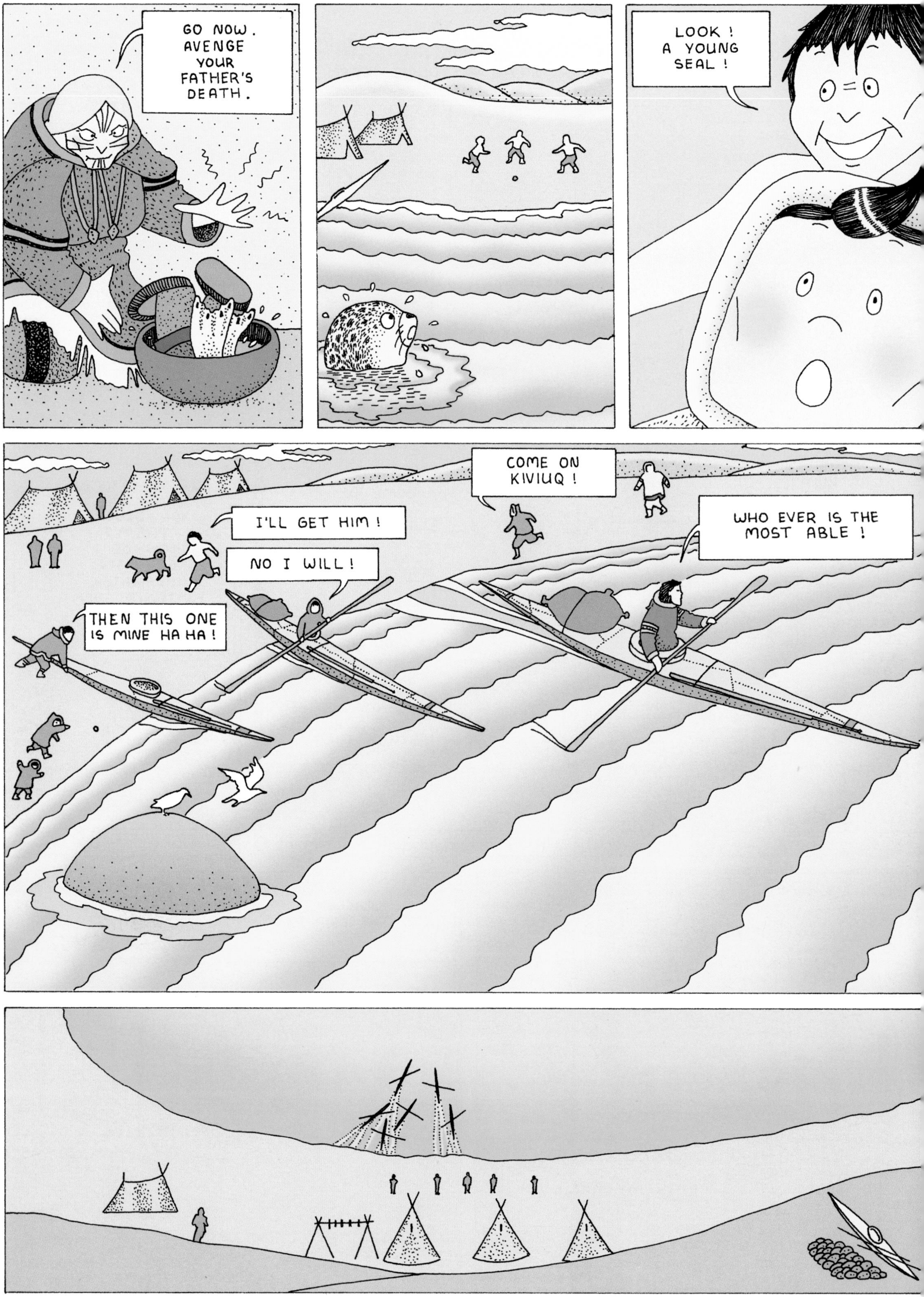
GO NOW. AVENGE YOUR FATHER'S DEATH.
LOOK! A YOUNG SEAL!
COME ON KIVIUQ!
I'LL GET HIM!
NO I WILL!
WHO EVER IS THE MOST ABLE!
THEN THIS ONE IS MINE HA HA!

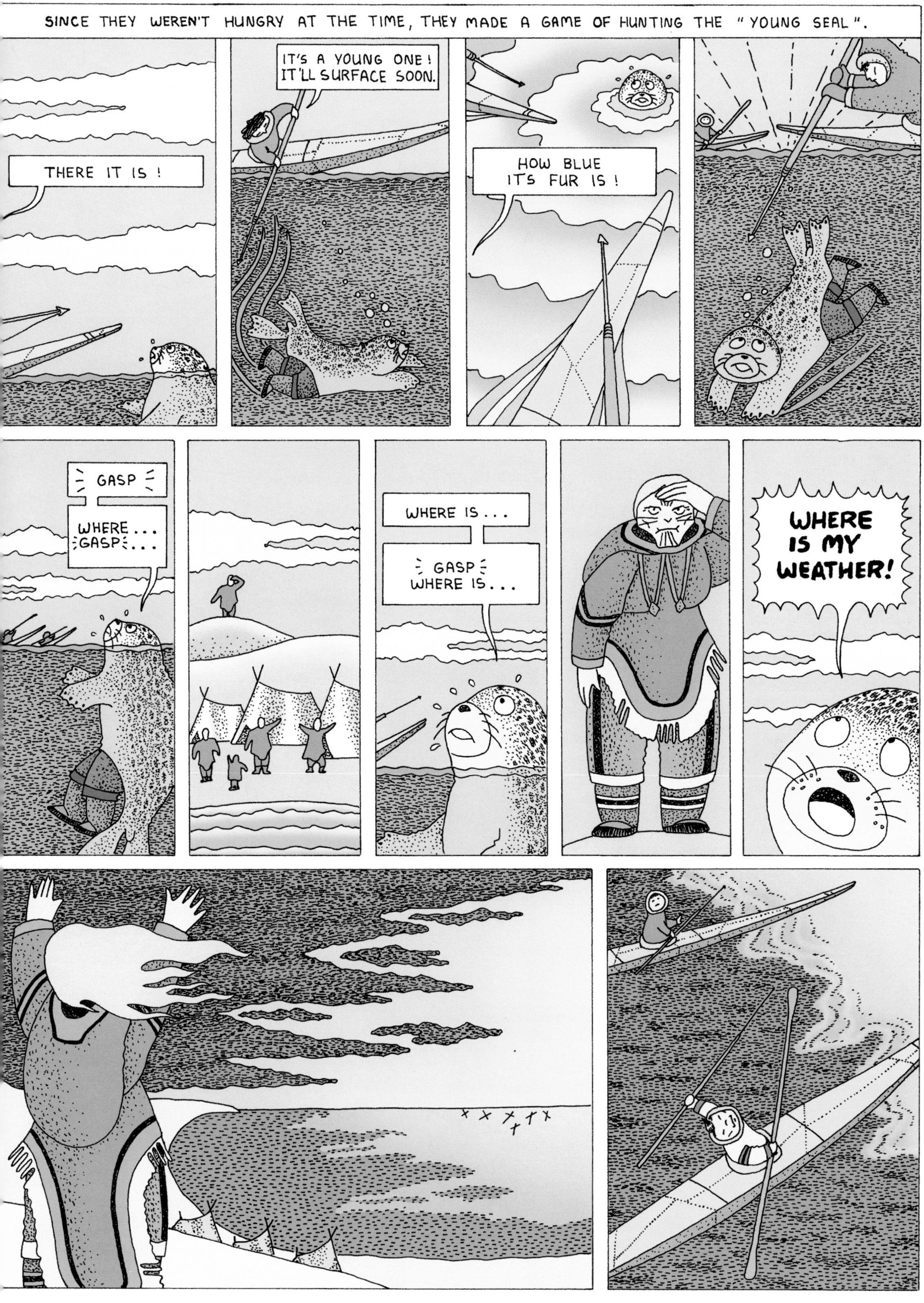
SINCE THEY WEREN'T HUNGRY AT THE TIME, THEY MADE A GAME OF HUNTING THE "YOUNG SEAL".
THERE IT IS !
IT'S A YOUNG ONE! IT'LL SURFACE SOON.
HOW BLUE IT'S FUR IS !
GASP
WHERE... GASP...
WHERE IS...
GASP WHERE IS...
WHERE IS MY WEATHER!

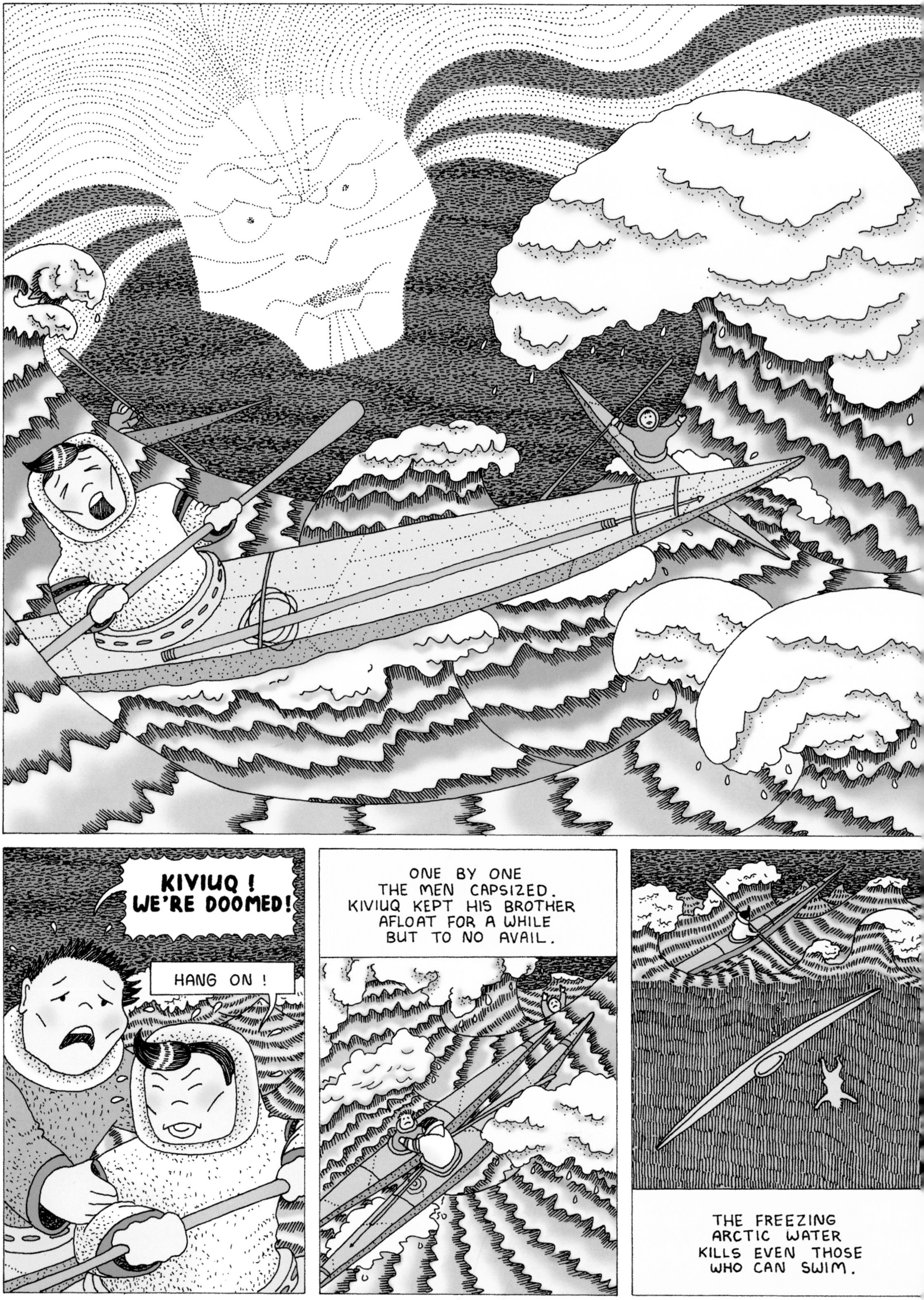
KIVIUQ ! WE'RE DOOMED!
HANG ON !
ONE BY ONE THE MEN CAPSIZED. KIVIUQ KEPT HIS BROTHER AFLOAT FOR A WHILE BUT TO NO AVAIL.
THE FREEZING ARCTIC WATER KILLS EVEN THOSE WHO CAN SWIM.

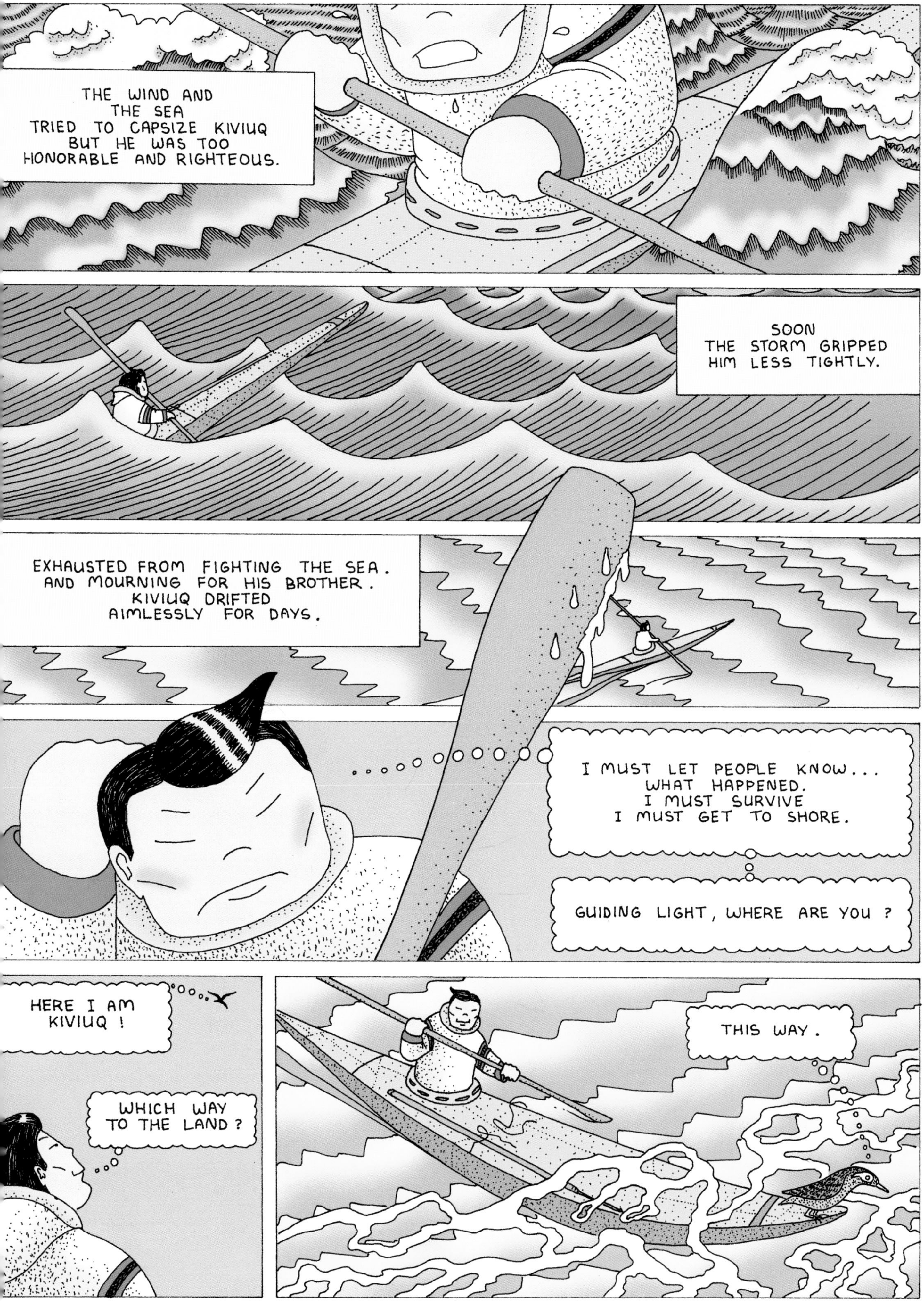
THE WIND AND THE SEA TRIED TO CAPSIZE KIVIUQ BUT HE WAS TOO HONORABLE AND RIGHTEOUS.
SOON THE STORM GRIPPED HIM LESS TIGHTLY.
EXHAUSTED FROM FIGHTING THE SEA. AND MOURNING FOR HIS BROTHER. KIVIUQ DRIFTED AIMLESSLY FOR DAYS.
I MUST LET PEOPLE KNOW... WHAT HAPPENED. I MUST SURVIVE I MUST GET TO SHORE.
GUIDING LIGHT, WHERE ARE YOU ?
HERE I AM KIVIUQ !
WHICH WAY TO THE LAND ?
THIS WAY.

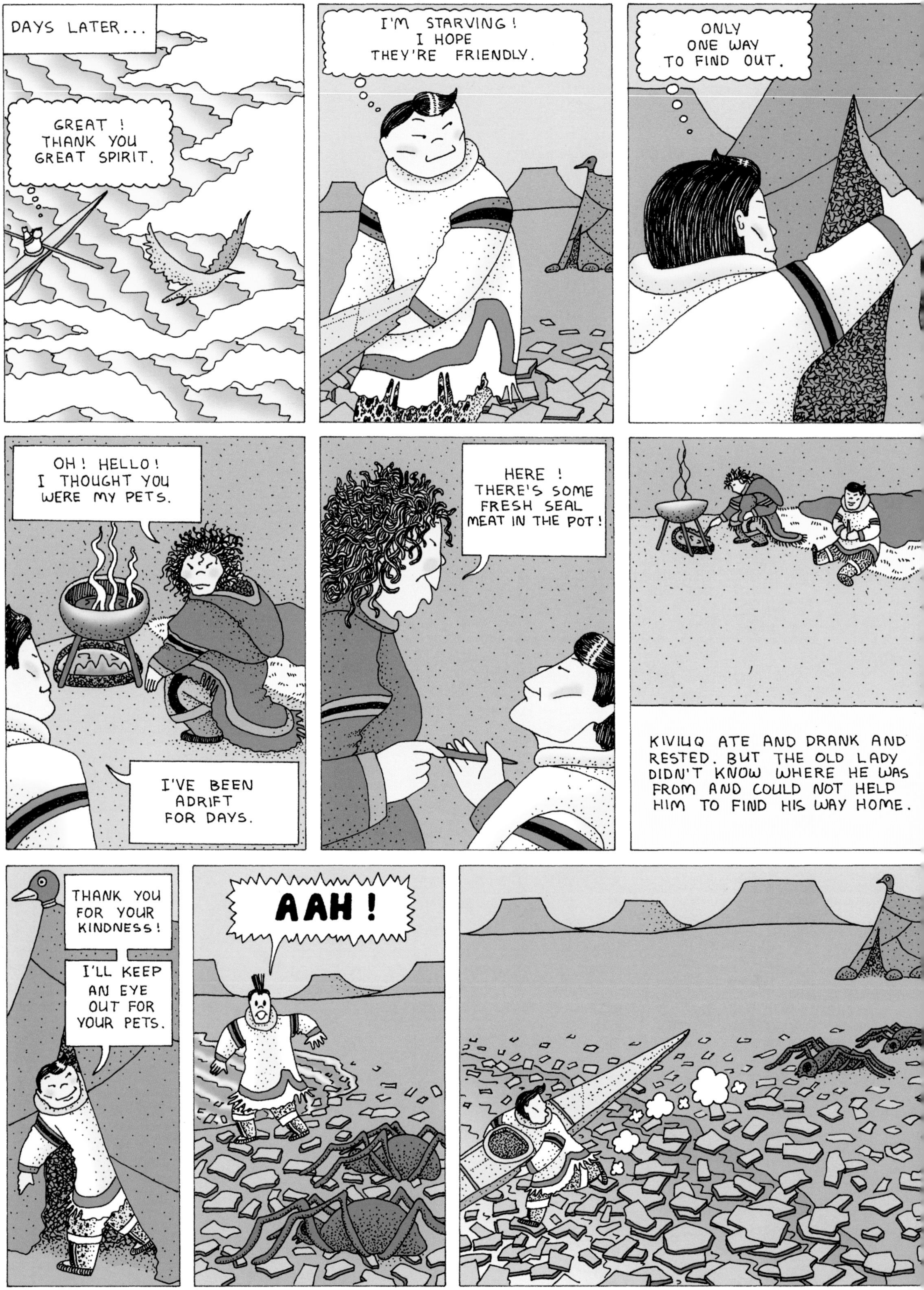
DAYS LATER...
GREAT ! THANK YOU GREAT SPIRIT.
I'M STARVING ! I HOPE THEY'RE FRIENDLY.
ONLY ONE WAY TO FIND OUT.
OH ! HELLO ! I THOUGHT YOU WERE MY PETS.
I'VE BEEN ADRIFT FOR DAYS.
HERE ! THERE'S SOME FRESH SEAL MEAT IN THE POT !
KIVIUQ ATE AND DRANK AND RESTED. BUT THE OLD LADY DIDN'T KNOW WHERE HE WAS FROM AND COULD NOT HELP HIM TO FIND HIS WAY HOME.
THANK YOU FOR YOUR KINDNESS !
I'LL KEEP AN EYE OUT FOR YOUR PETS.
AAH !

KIVIUQ PADDLED ALONG THE COAST FOR DAYS...
STRANGE ! ICE IS STILL HERE.
I MUST BE GOING IN THE WRONG DIRECTION.
MAYBE THESE PEOPLE CAN HELP ME GET MY BEARINGS.
NO DOOR ?
NO ROOF EITHER !
SHE'S VERY BUSY SCRAPING THAT BEAR SKIN.
I'LL HAVE SOME FUN.
?
OH!
I HAVEN'T HAD A DRIP ALL DAY AND THERE IT IS FINALLY !

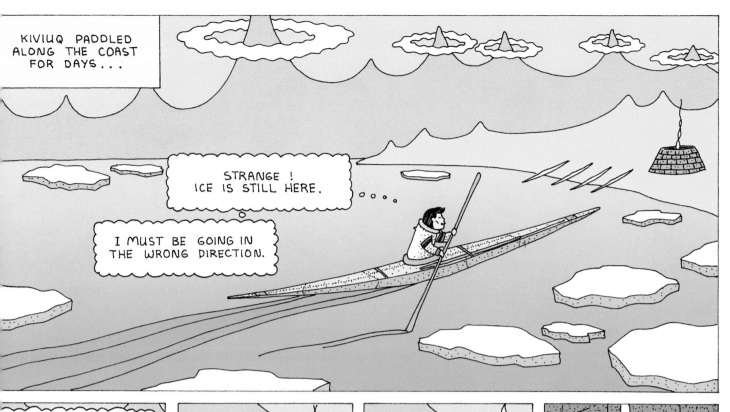

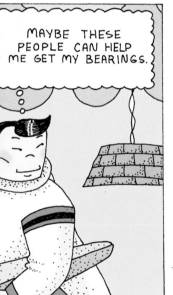

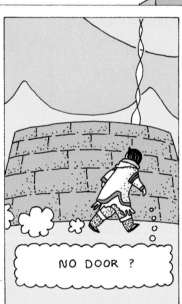

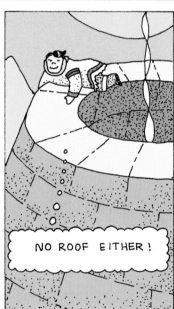

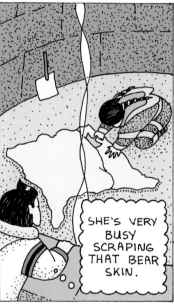

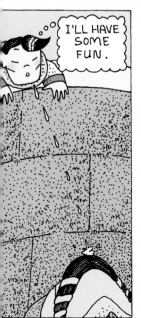

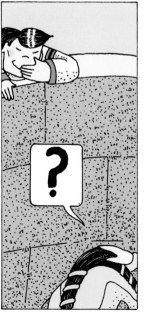

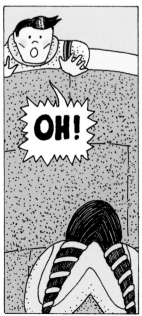

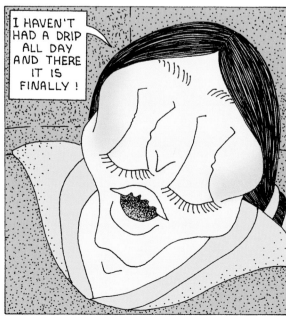

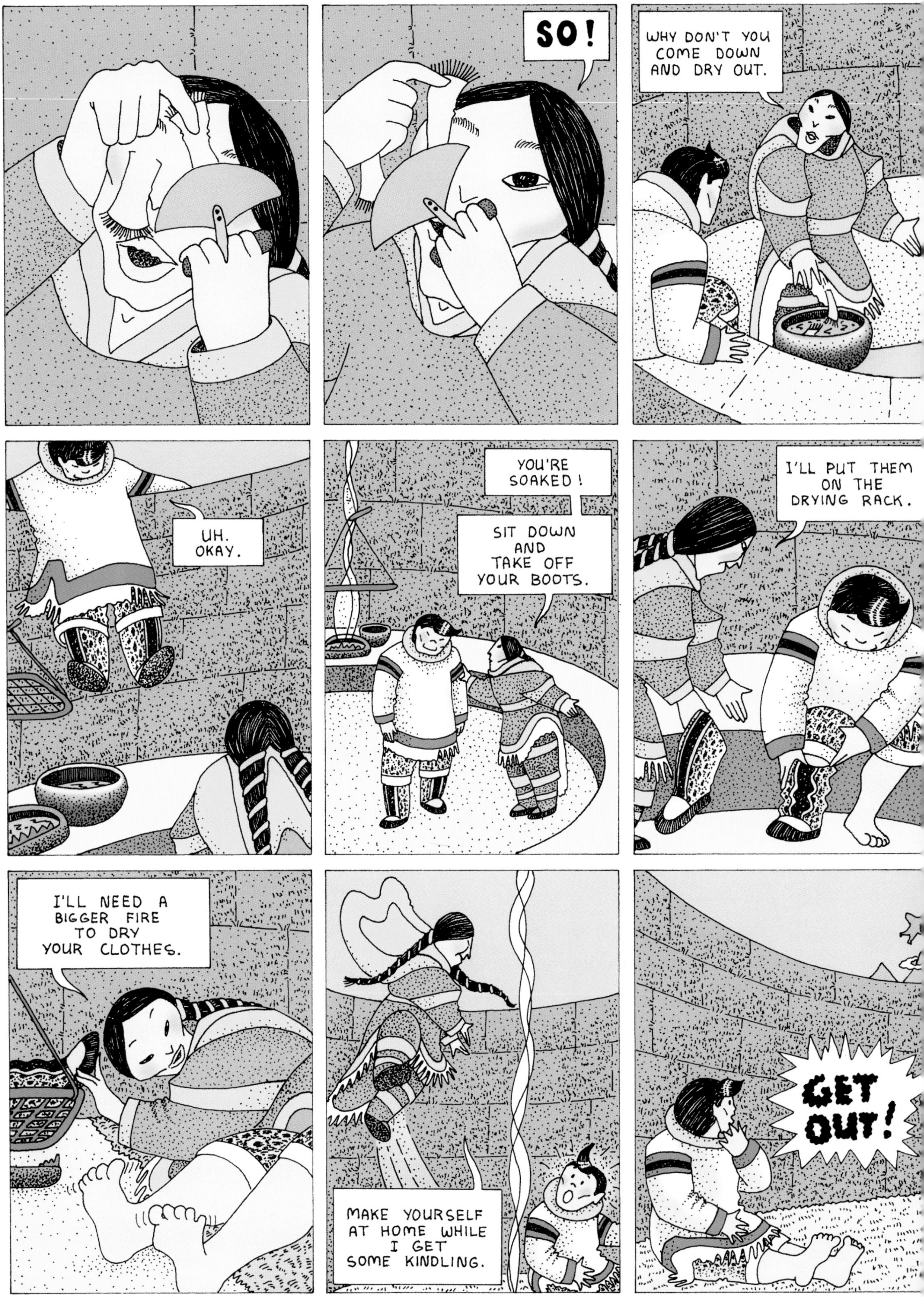
SO!
WHY DON'T YOU COME DOWN AND DRY OUT.
UH. OKAY.
YOU'RE SOAKED!
SIT DOWN AND TAKE OFF YOUR BOOTS.
I'LL PUT THEM ON THE DRYING RACK.
I'LL NEED A BIGGER FIRE TO DRY YOUR CLOTHES.
MAKE YOURSELF AT HOME WHILE I GET SOME KINDLING.
GET OUT!

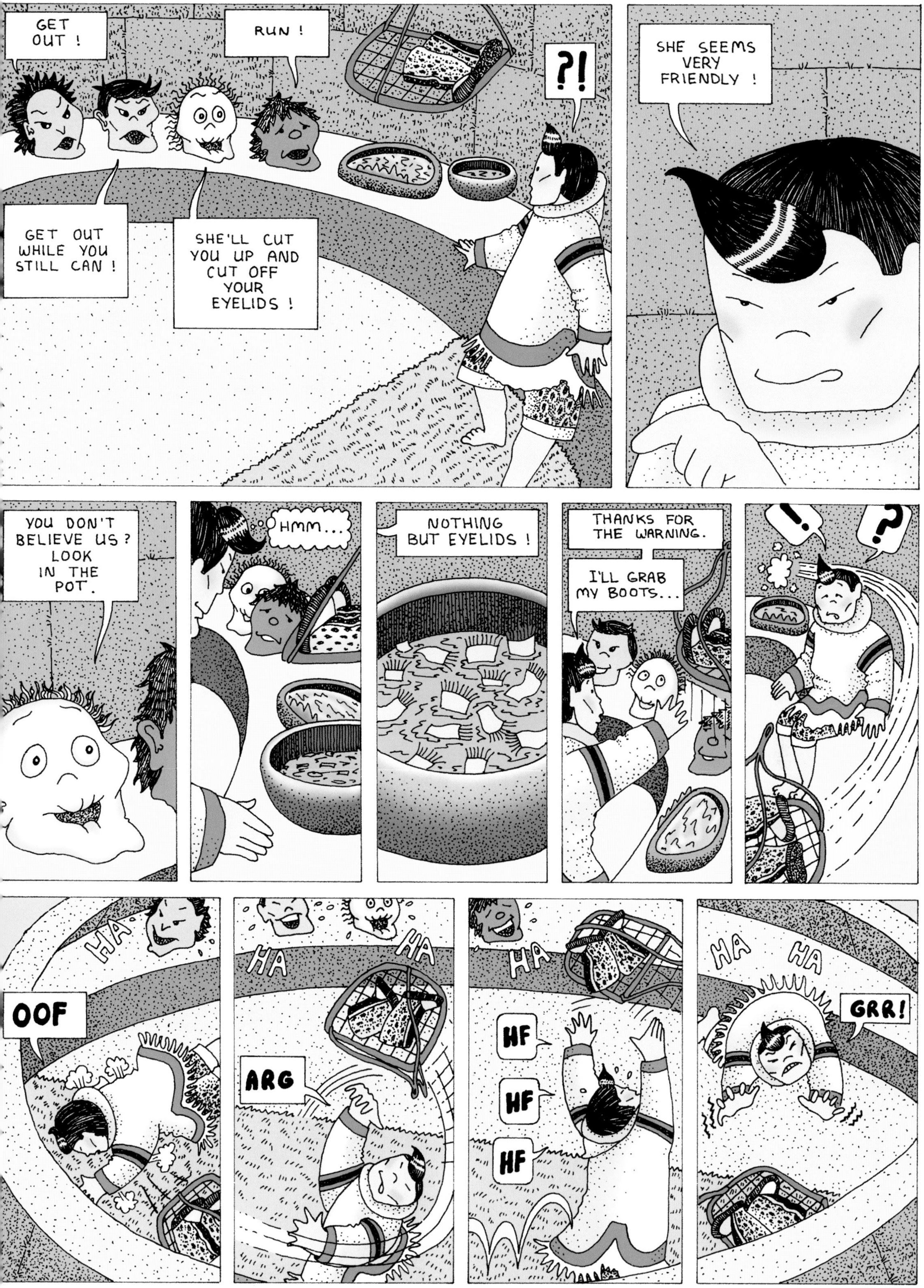
GET OUT !
RUN !
?!
GET OUT WHILE YOU STILL CAN !
SHE'LL CUT YOU UP AND CUT OFF YOUR EYELIDS !
SHE SEEMS VERY FRIENDLY !
YOU DON'T BELIEVE US ? LOOK IN THE POT.
HMM...
NOTHING BUT EYELIDS !
THANKS FOR THE WARNING.
I'LL GRAB MY BOOTS...
!
?
HA
OOF
HA
HA
ARG
HA
HF
HF
HF
HA
HA
GRR!

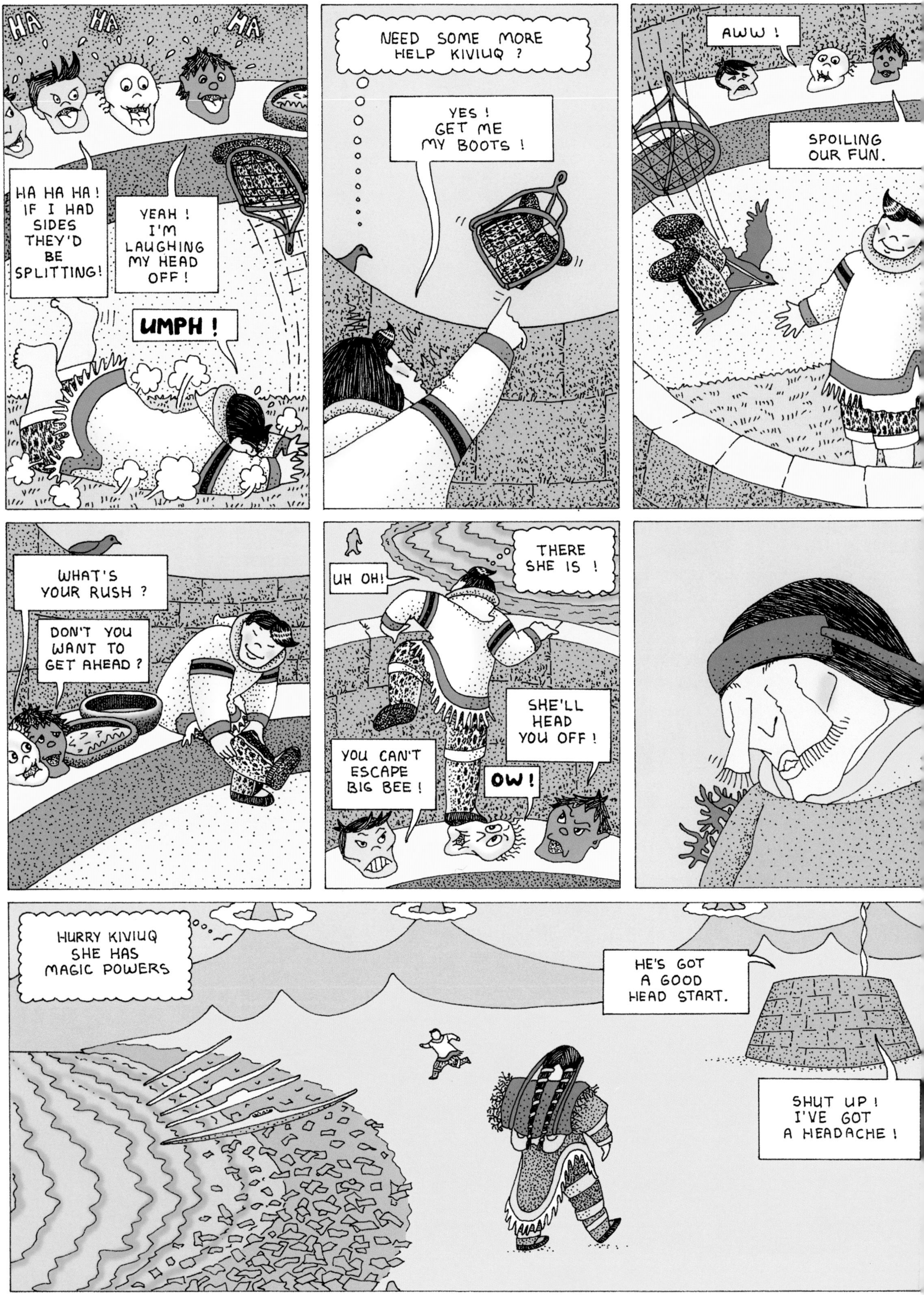

HA HA HA
HA HA HA! IF I HAD SIDES THEY'D BE SPLITTING!
YEAH! I'M LAUGHING MY HEAD OFF!
UMPH!
NEED SOME MORE HELP KIVIUQ?
YES! GET ME MY BOOTS!
AWW!
SPOILING OUR FUN.
WHAT'S YOUR RUSH?
DON'T YOU WANT TO GET AHEAD?
UH OH!
THERE SHE IS!
SHE'LL HEAD YOU OFF!
YOU CAN'T ESCAPE BIG BEE!
OW!
HURRY KIVIUQ SHE HAS MAGIC POWERS
HE'S GOT A GOOD HEAD START.
SHUT UP! I'VE GOT A HEADACHE!

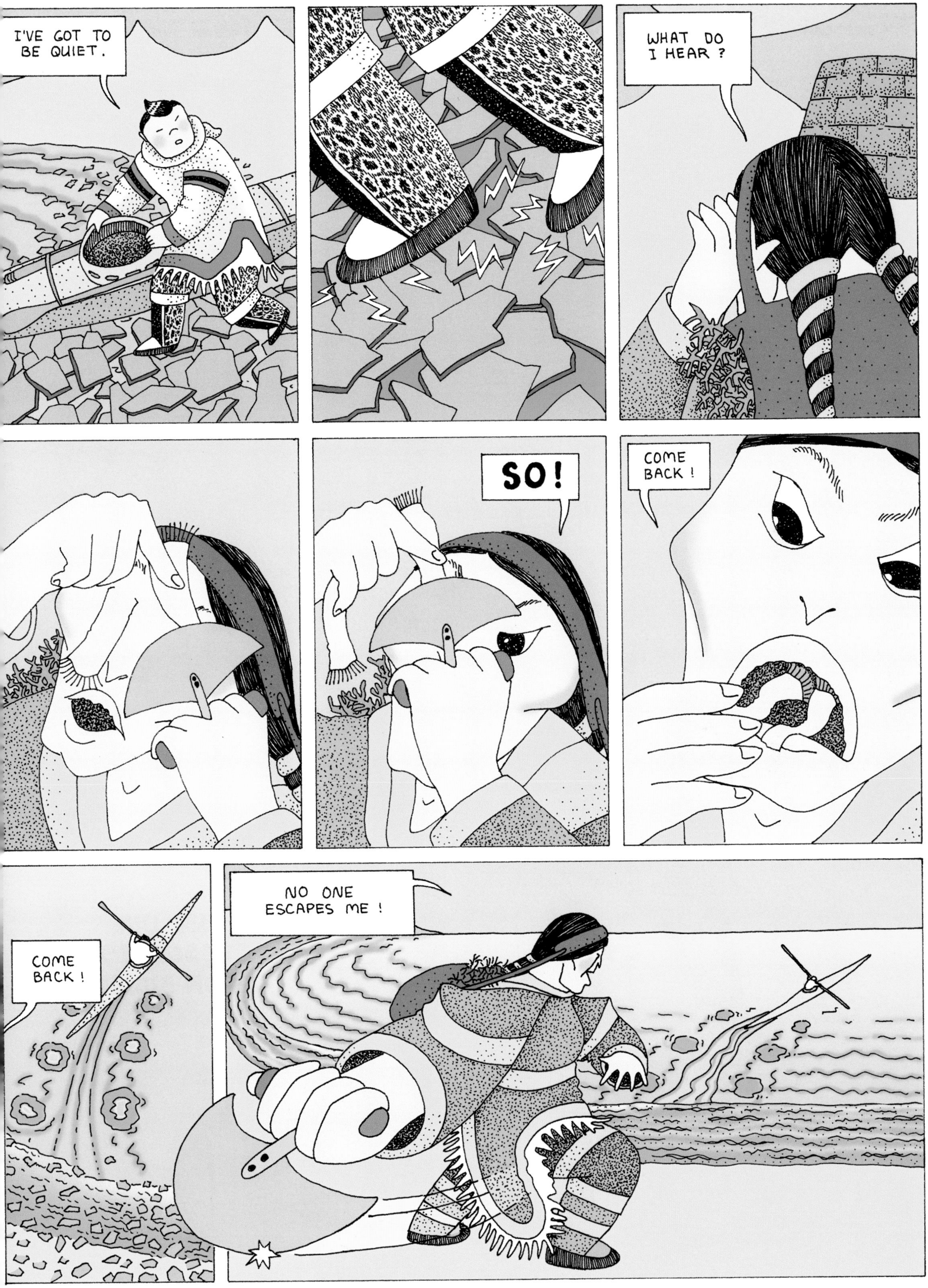
I'VE GOT TO BE QUIET.
WHAT DO I HEAR ?
SO!
COME BACK !
COME BACK !
NO ONE ESCAPES ME !

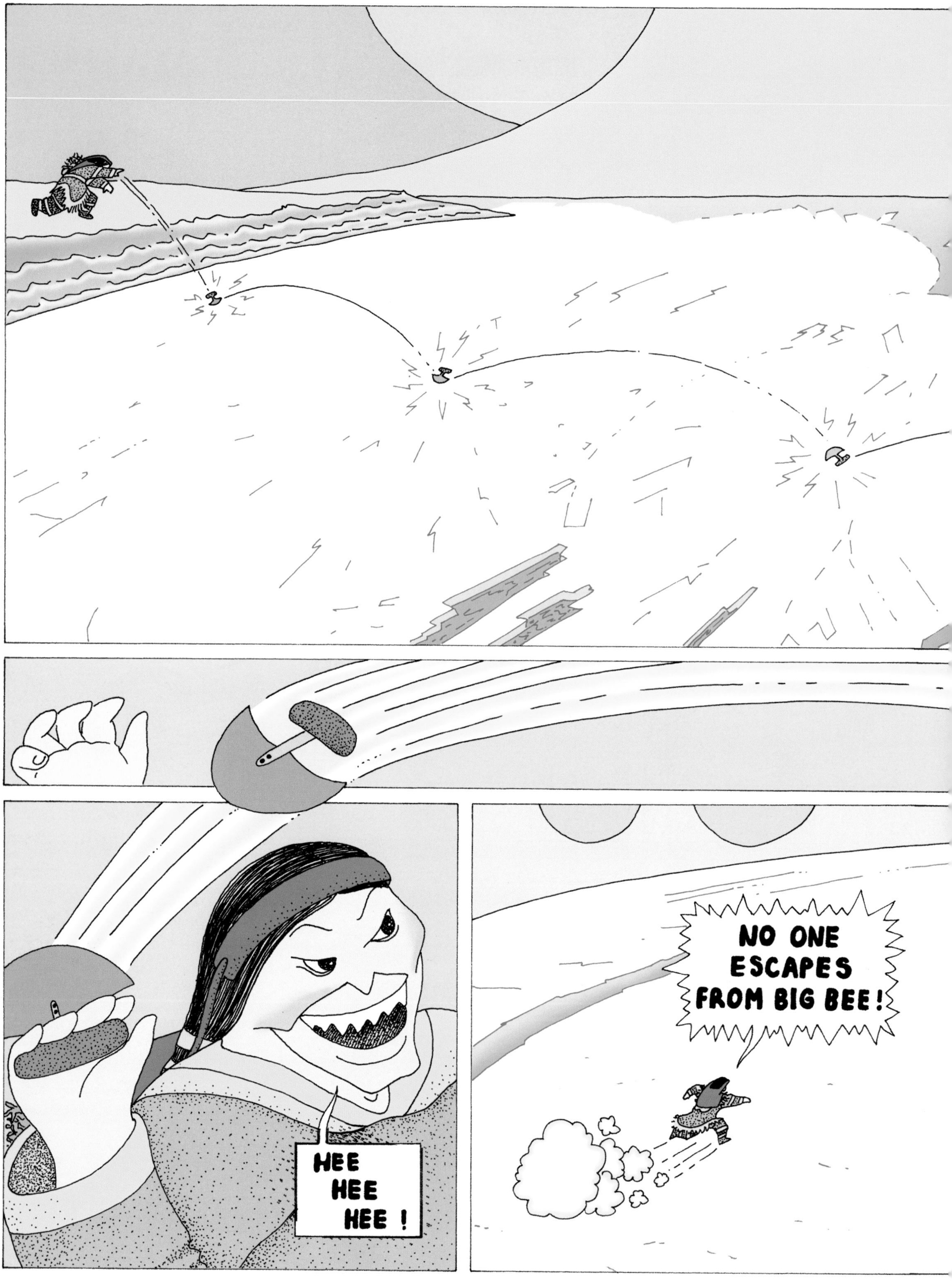
HEE HEE HEE !
NO ONE ESCAPES FROM BIG BEE !

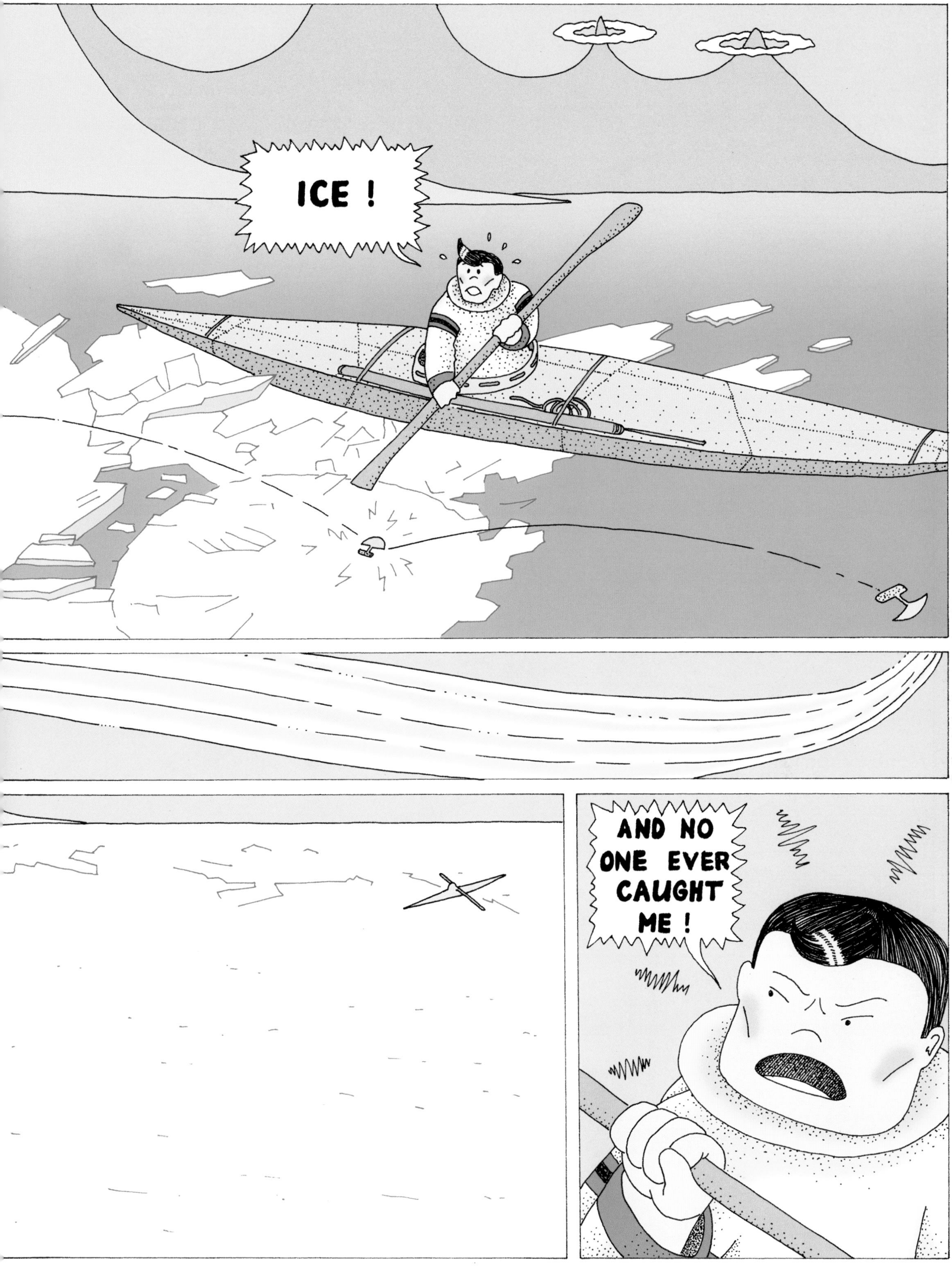
ICE !
AND NO ONE EVER CAUGHT ME !

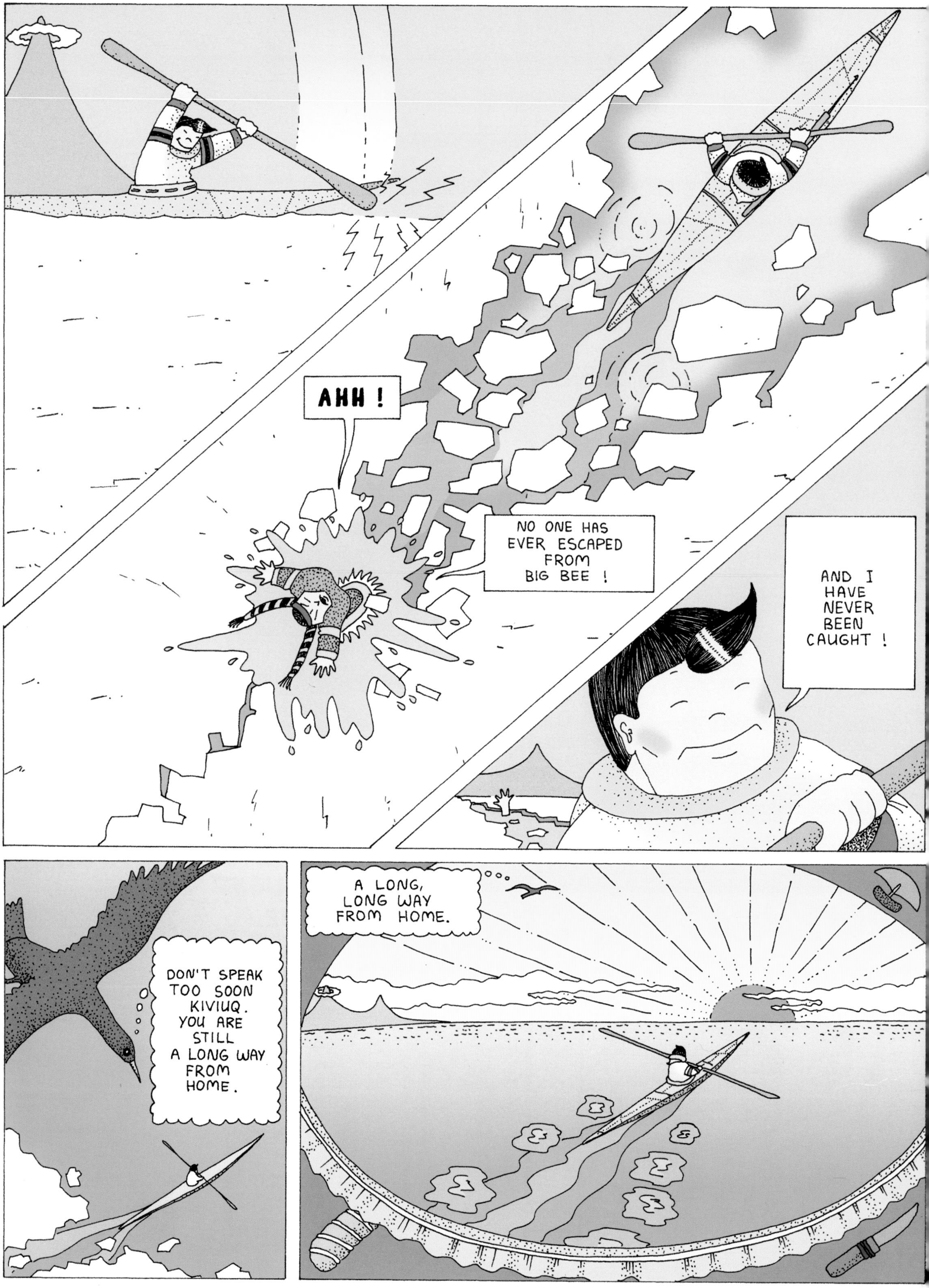
AHH !
NO ONE HAS EVER ESCAPED FROM BIG BEE !
AND I HAVE NEVER BEEN CAUGHT !
DON'T SPEAK TOO SOON KIVIUQ. YOU ARE STILL A LONG WAY FROM HOME.
A LONG, LONG WAY FROM HOME.

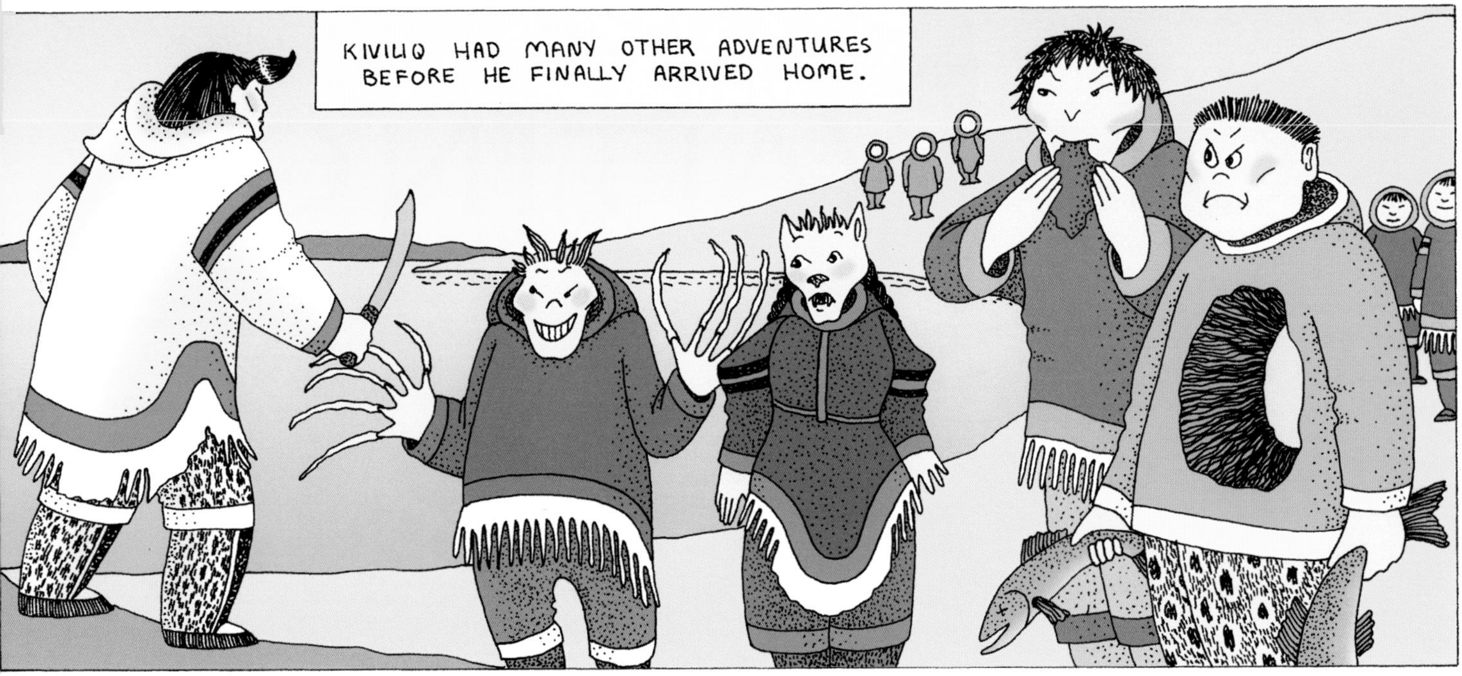
KIVIUQ HAD MANY OTHER ADVENTURES BEFORE HE FINALLY ARRIVED HOME.

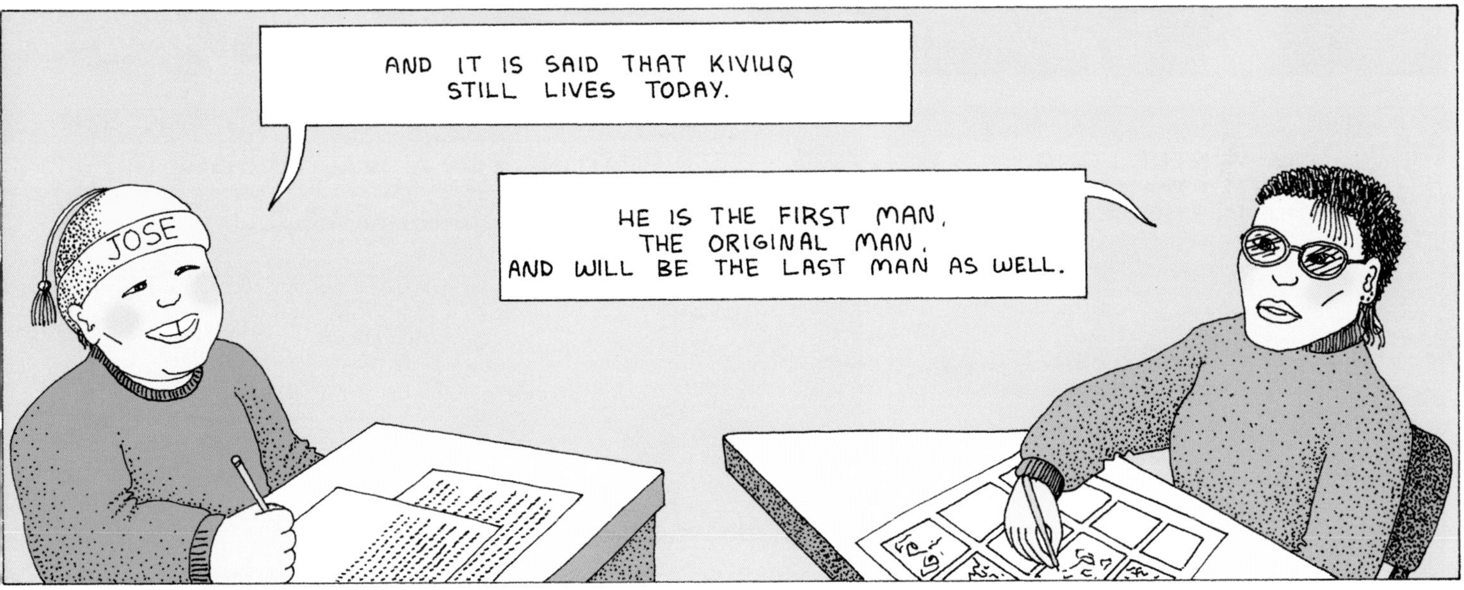
AND IT IS SAID THAT KIVIUQ STILL LIVES TODAY.
HE IS THE FIRST MAN, THE ORIGINAL MAN, AND WILL BE THE LAST MAN AS WELL.
JOSE

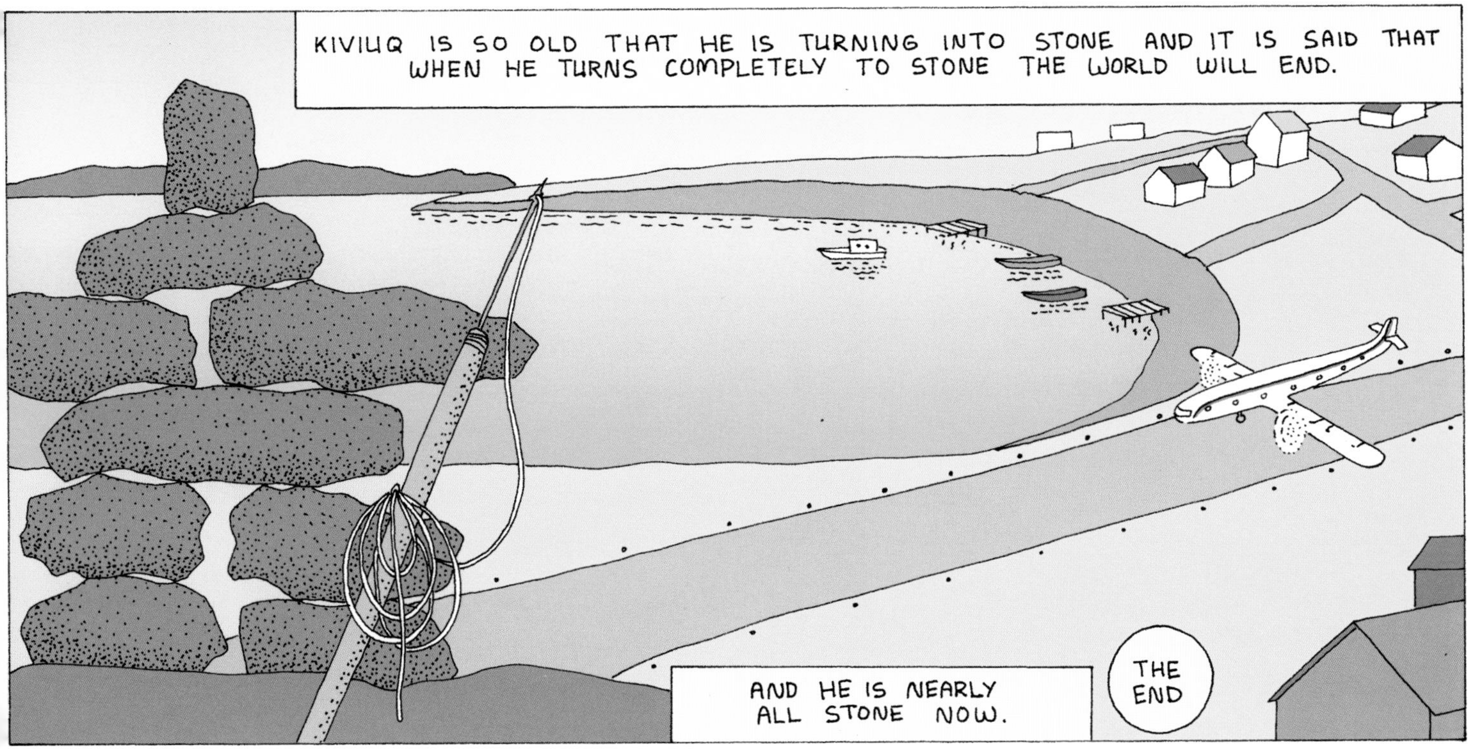
KIVIUQ IS SO OLD THAT HE IS TURNING INTO STONE AND IT IS SAID THAT WHEN HE TURNS COMPLETELY TO STONE THE WORLD WILL END.
AND HE IS NEARLY ALL STONE NOW.
THE END

ON WAITING

ALL WINTER LONG. PATIENTLY WAITING AT A HOLE IN THE SEA ICE.

FOR HOURS.

WAITING FOR A SEAL TO COME UP.

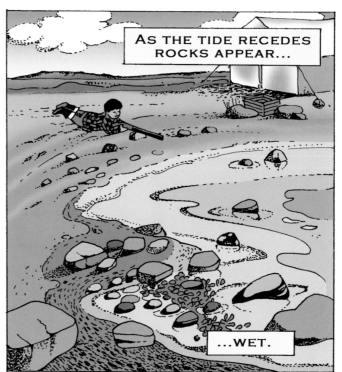

AS THE TIDE RECEDES ROCKS APPEAR...

...WET.

①

WE WAIT AND WE WAIT...

...FOR SEALS TO SURFACE.

ALL SUMMER LONG.

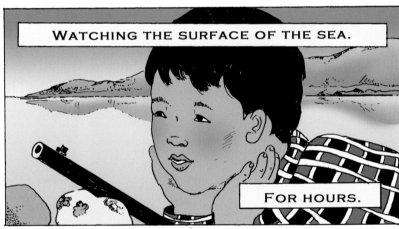

WATCHING THE SURFACE OF THE SEA.

FOR HOURS.

TINY WAVES LAPPING ON THE ROCKS...

...CLIMBING UP THE BEACH, ONLY TO RECEDE AGAIN...

...WAVING THE SEAWEEDS.

TINY JELLYFISH COME AND GO.

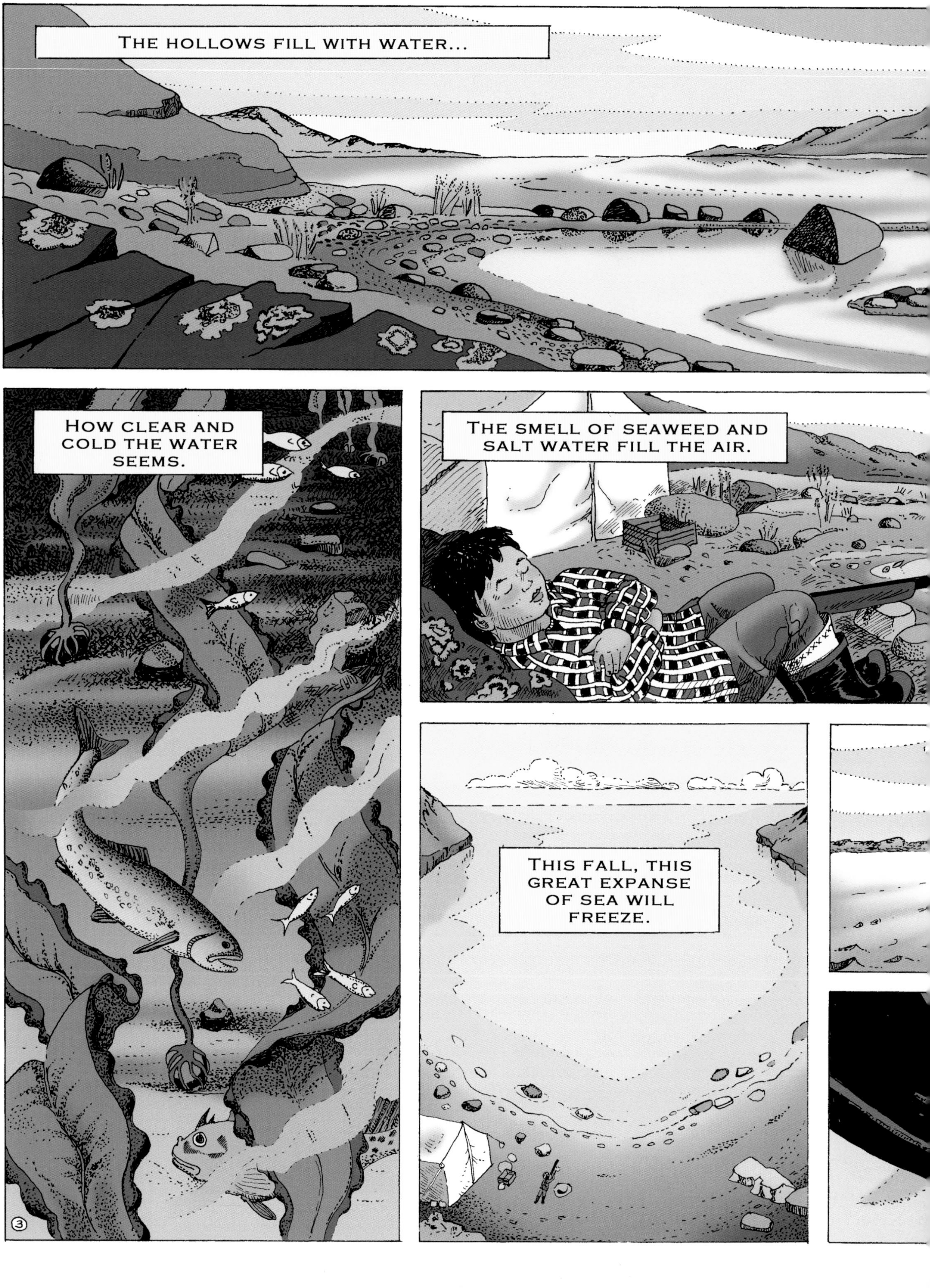
THE HOLLOWS FILL WITH WATER...
HOW CLEAR AND COLD THE WATER SEEMS.
THE SMELL OF SEAWEED AND SALT WATER FILL THE AIR.
THIS FALL, THIS GREAT EXPANSE OF SEA WILL FREEZE.

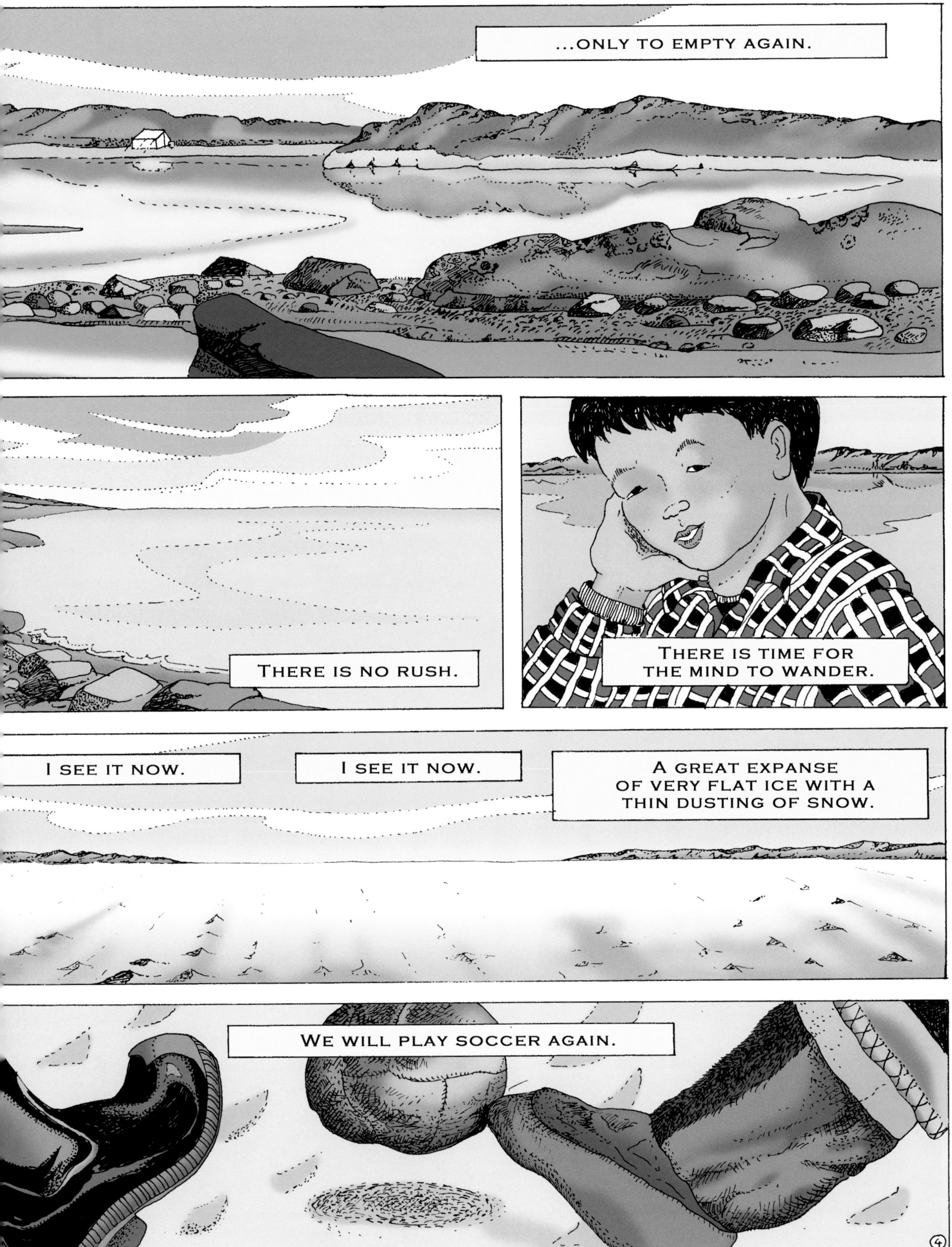
...ONLY TO EMPTY AGAIN.
THERE IS NO RUSH.
THERE IS TIME FOR THE MIND TO WANDER.
I SEE IT NOW.
I SEE IT NOW.
A GREAT EXPANSE OF VERY FLAT ICE WITH A THIN DUSTING OF SNOW.
WE WILL PLAY SOCCER AGAIN.
4

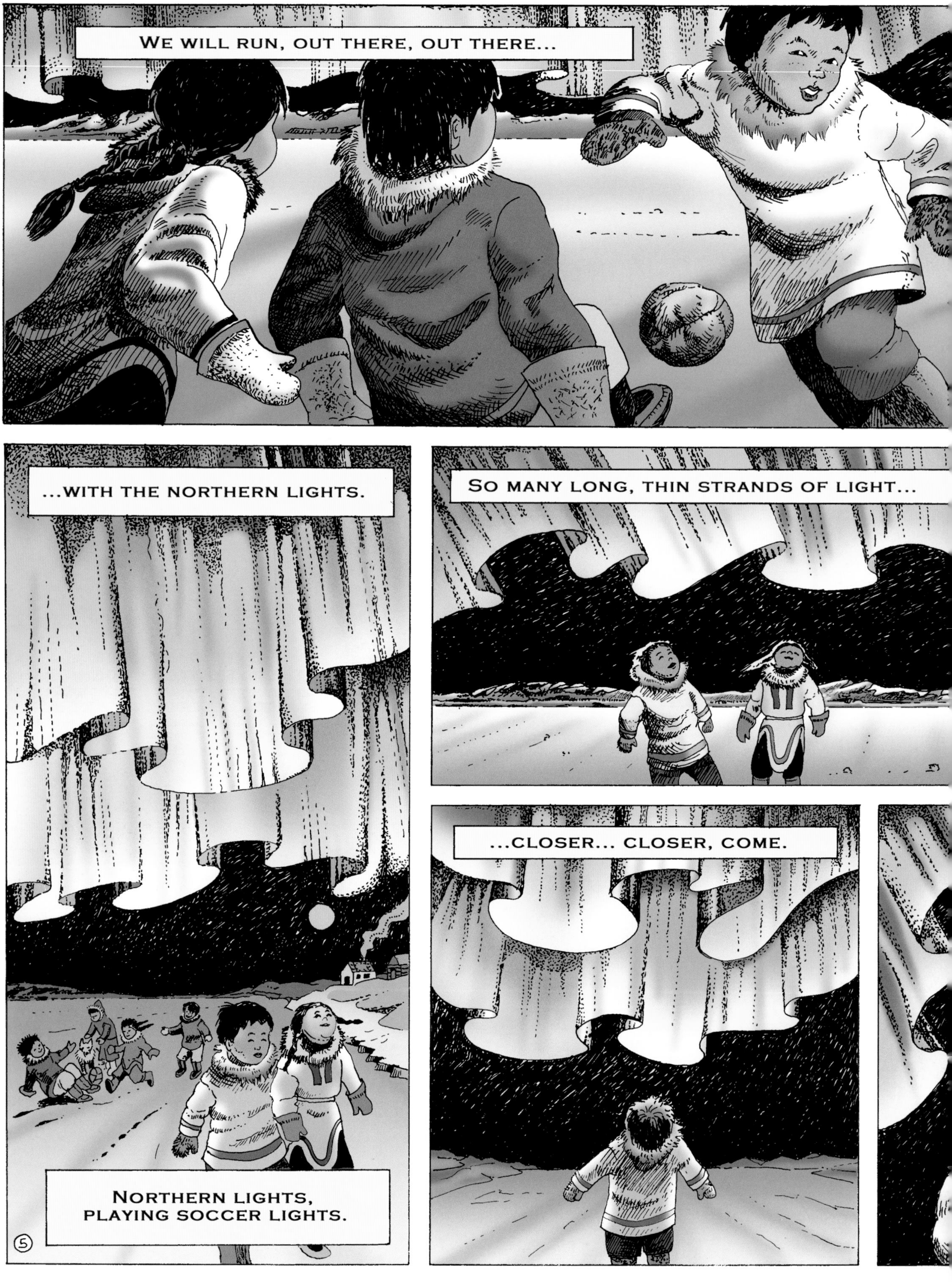
We will run, out there, out there...
...with the northern lights.
Northern lights, playing soccer lights.
So many long, thin strands of light...
...closer... closer, come.

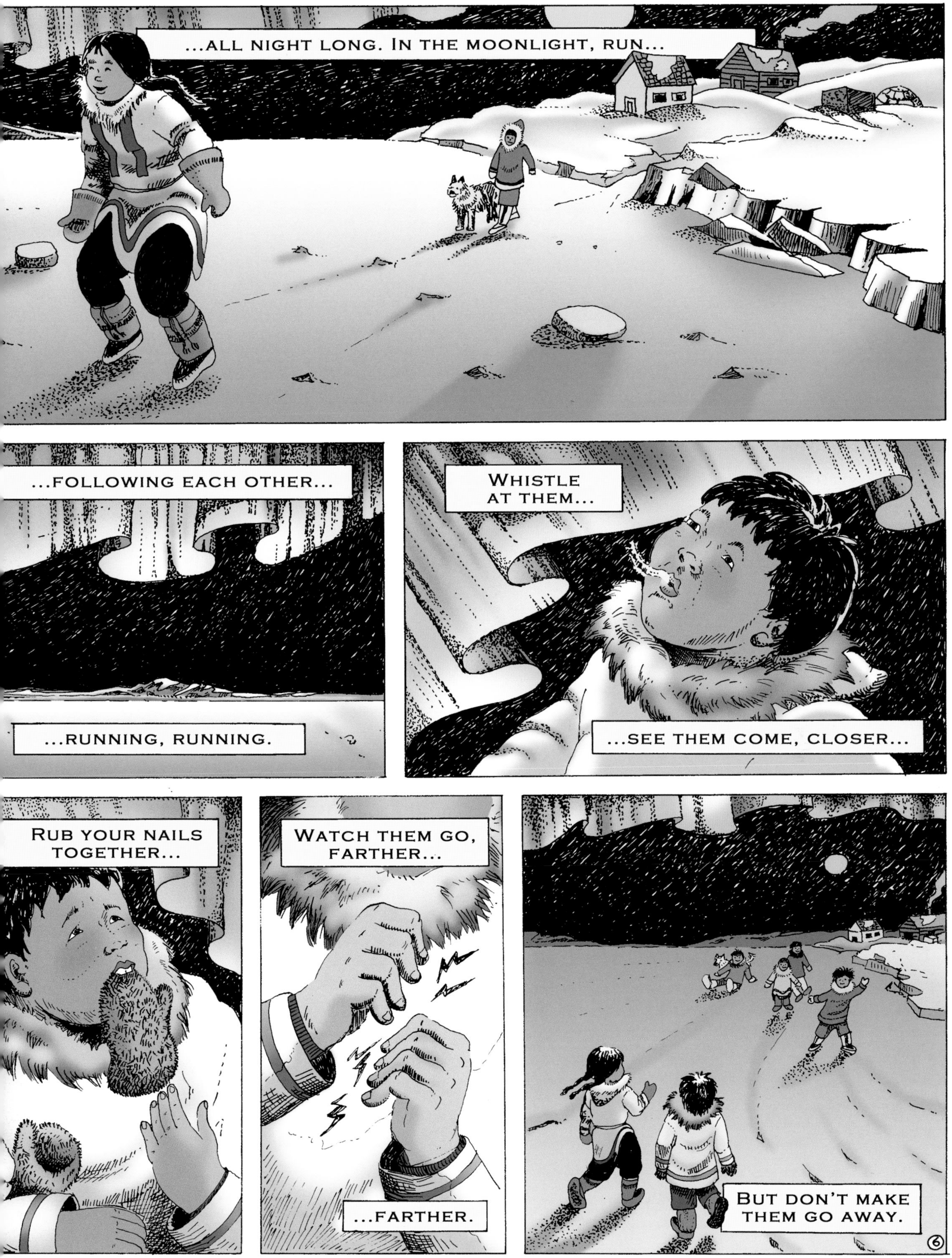
...ALL NIGHT LONG. IN THE MOONLIGHT, RUN...
...FOLLOWING EACH OTHER...
...RUNNING, RUNNING.
WHISTLE AT THEM...
...SEE THEM COME, CLOSER...
RUB YOUR NAILS TOGETHER...
WATCH THEM GO, FARTHER...
...FARTHER.
BUT DON'T MAKE THEM GO AWAY.

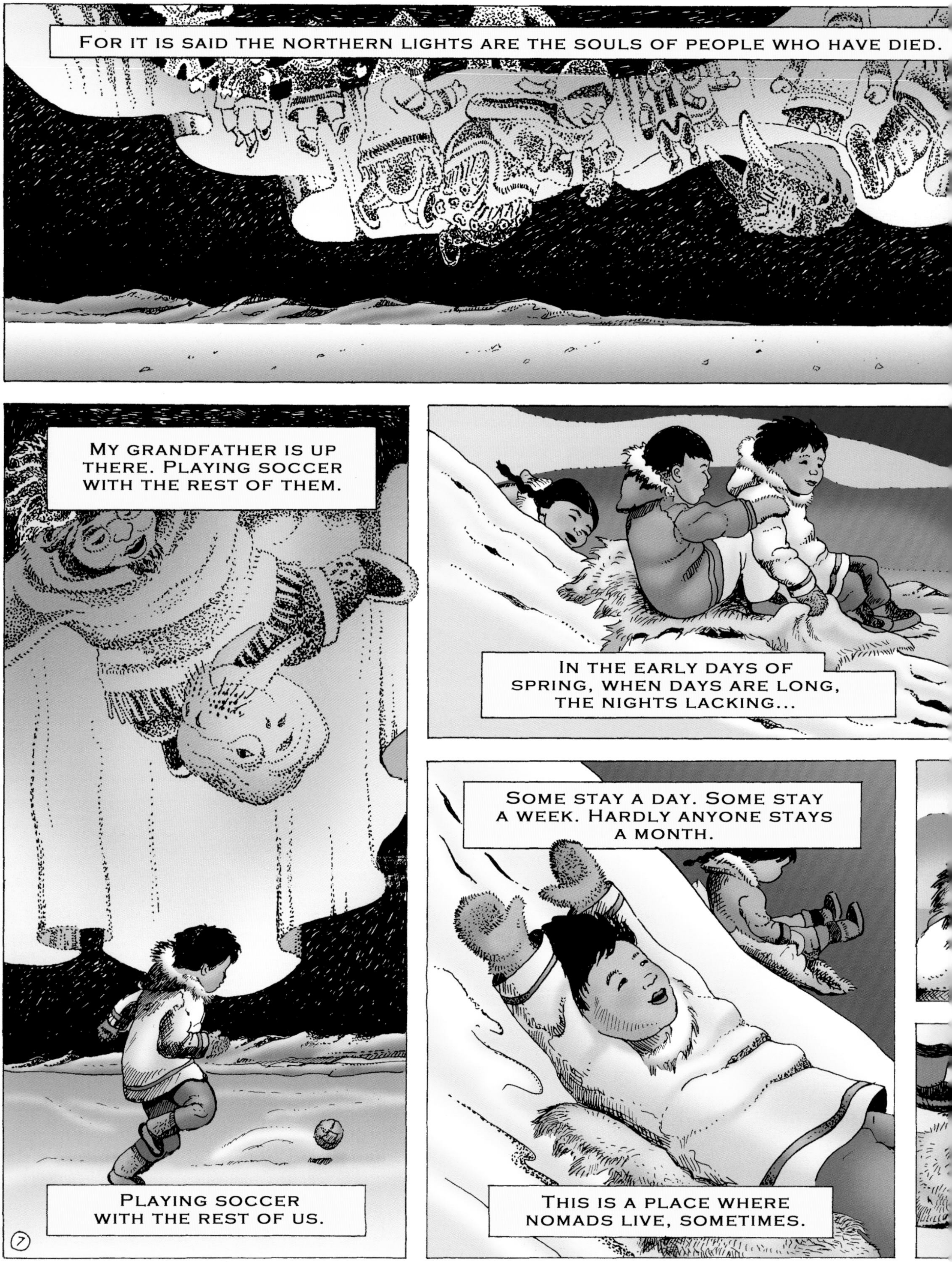
For it is said the northern lights are the souls of people who have died.
My grandfather is up there. Playing soccer with the rest of them.
Playing soccer with the rest of us.
In the early days of spring, when days are long, the nights lacking...
Some stay a day. Some stay a week. Hardly anyone stays a month.
This is a place where nomads live, sometimes.

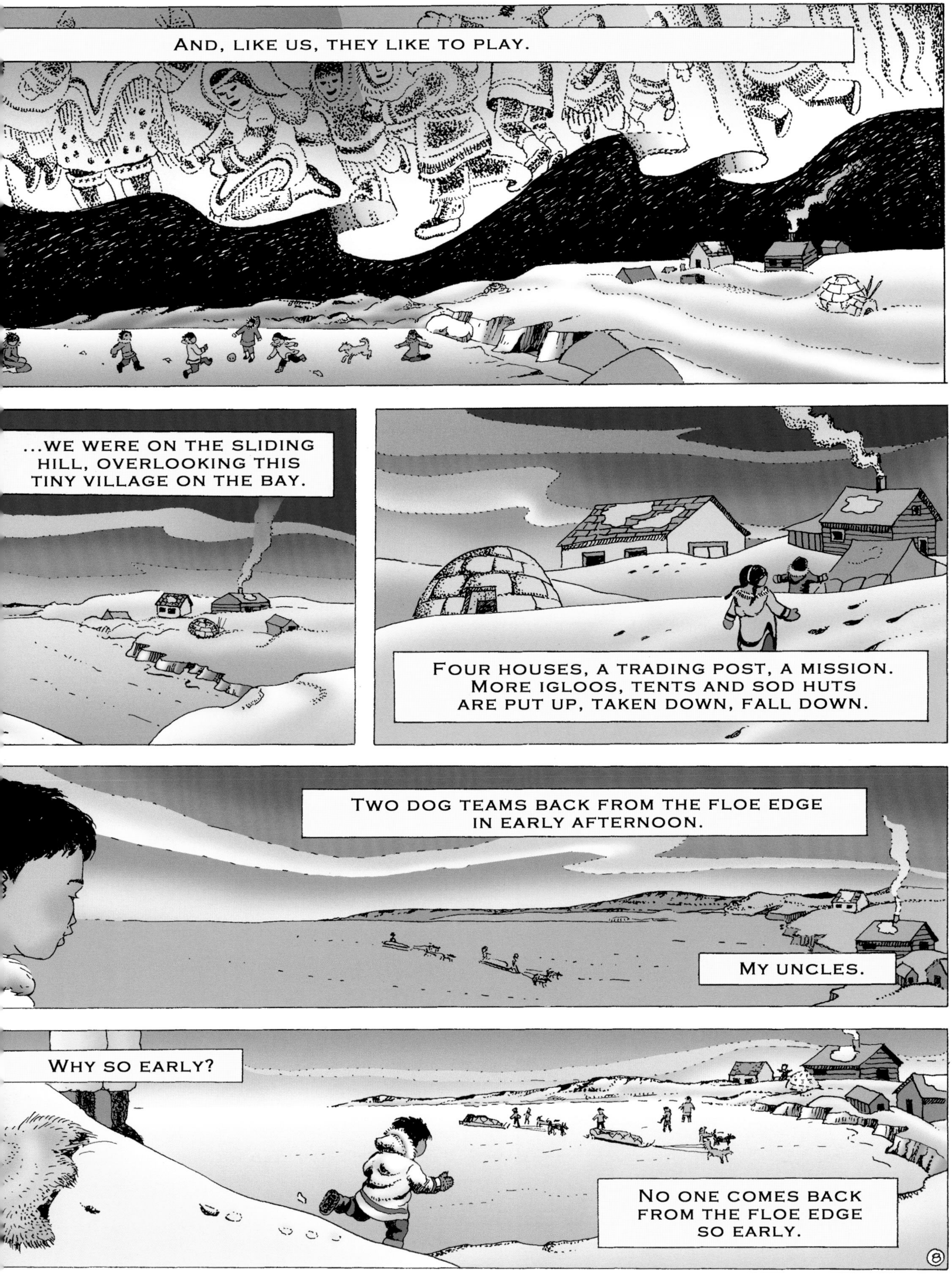

And, like us, they like to play.
...we were on the sliding hill, overlooking this tiny village on the bay.
Four houses, a trading post, a mission. More igloos, tents and sod huts are put up, taken down, fall down.
Two dog teams back from the floe edge in early afternoon.
My uncles.
Why so early?
No one comes back from the floe edge so early.

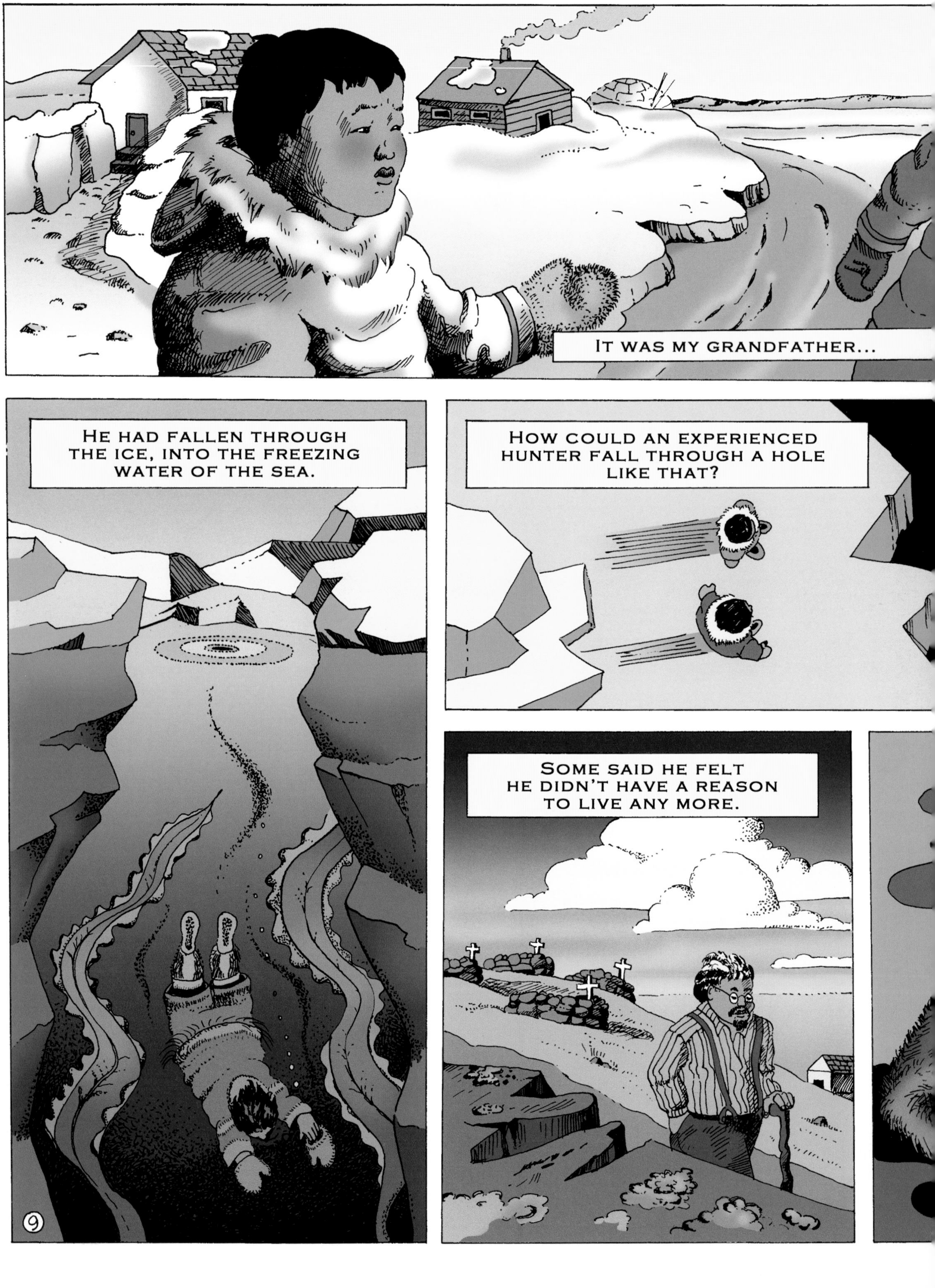
It was my grandfather...
He had fallen through the ice, into the freezing water of the sea.
How could an experienced hunter fall through a hole like that?
Some said he felt he didn't have a reason to live any more.

...LASHED UPON THE SLED.

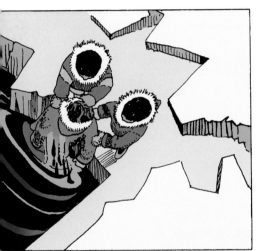

HIS WIFE WAS GONE, HIS SONS ALL GROWN...

...HIS DAUGHTERS BORE HIM GRANDCHILDREN, ALL.

AND HE DIDN'T TRY TO GET OUT.

FOR A LONG TIME I THOUGHT...

"WHAT ABOUT ME?"

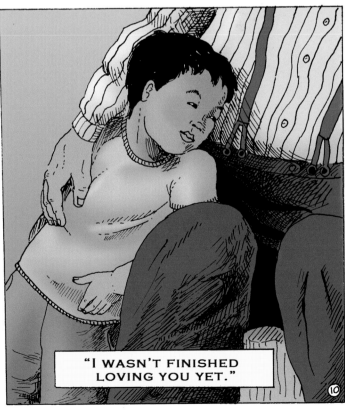

"I WASN'T FINISHED LOVING YOU YET."

10

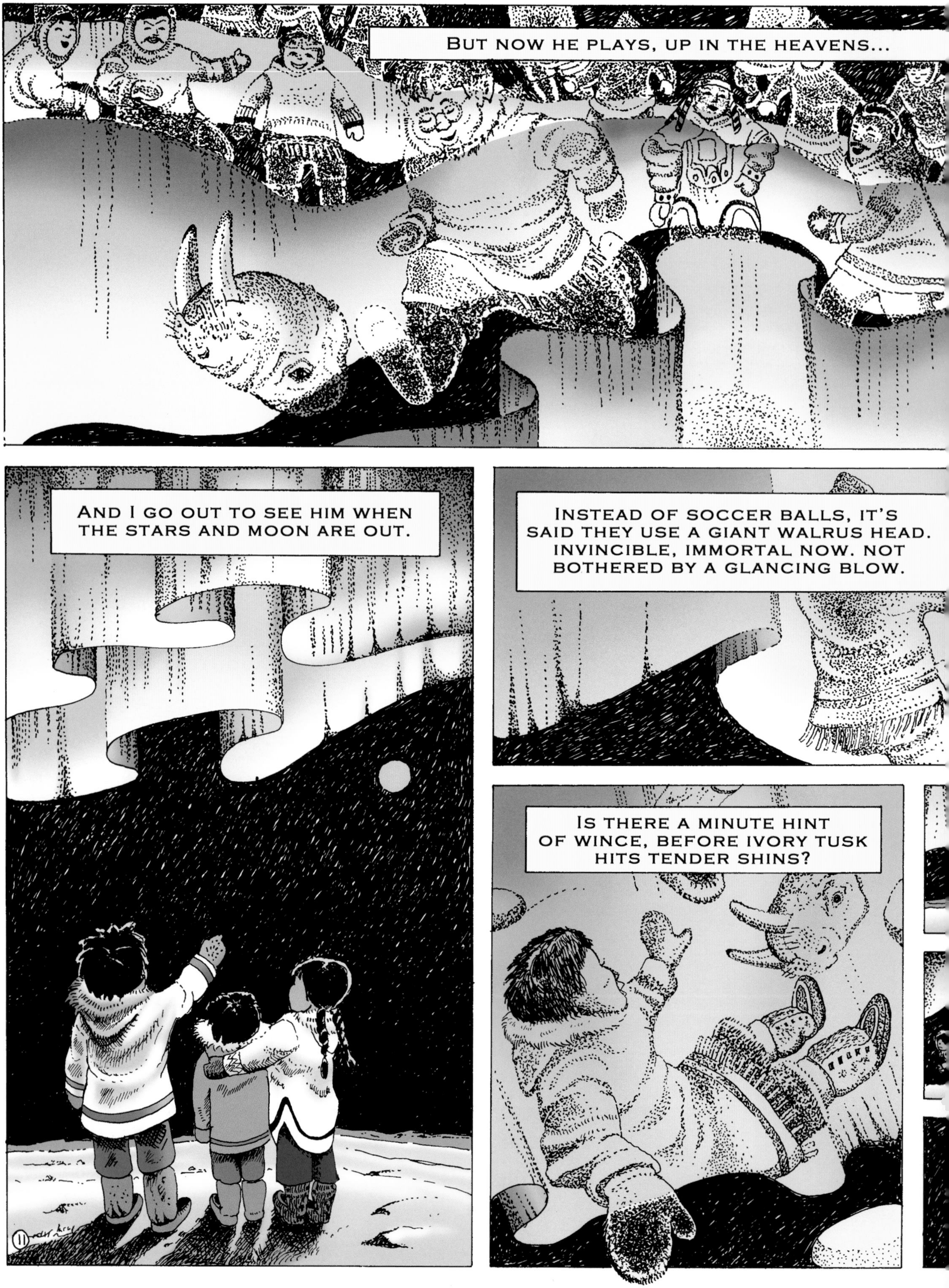

But now he plays, up in the heavens...
And I go out to see him when the stars and moon are out.
Instead of soccer balls, it's said they use a giant walrus head. Invincible, immortal now. Not bothered by a glancing blow.
Is there a minute hint of wince, before ivory tusk hits tender shins?

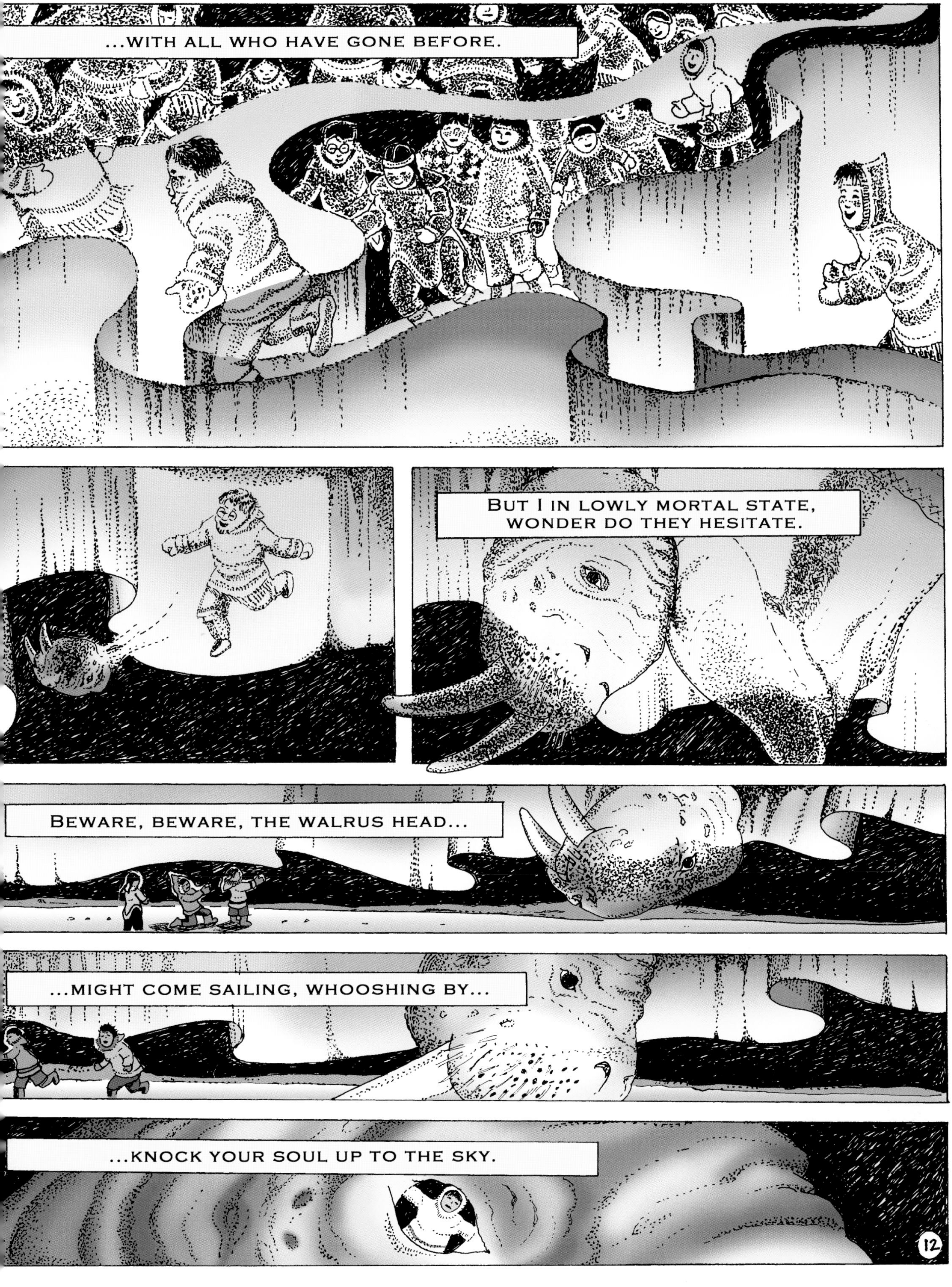
...WITH ALL WHO HAVE GONE BEFORE.
BUT I IN LOWLY MORTAL STATE, WONDER DO THEY HESITATE.
BEWARE, BEWARE, THE WALRUS HEAD...
...MIGHT COME SAILING, WHOOSHING BY...
...KNOCK YOUR SOUL UP TO THE SKY.

AH, THERE IS A SEAL...

PERHAPS IT WILL SURFACE AGAIN, A BIT CLOSER.

NO MATTER.

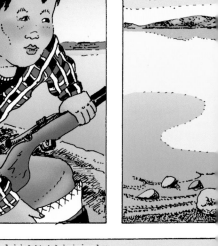

...TO WAIT...

⑬

...BUT IT IS TOO FAR.

I'LL COME AGAIN TOMORROW...

...FOR SEALS
TO SURFACE.

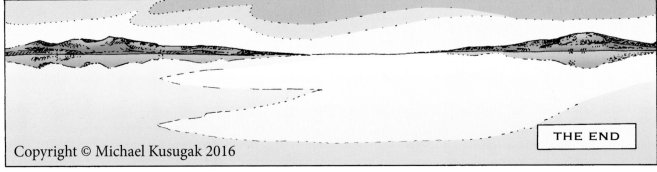

THE END

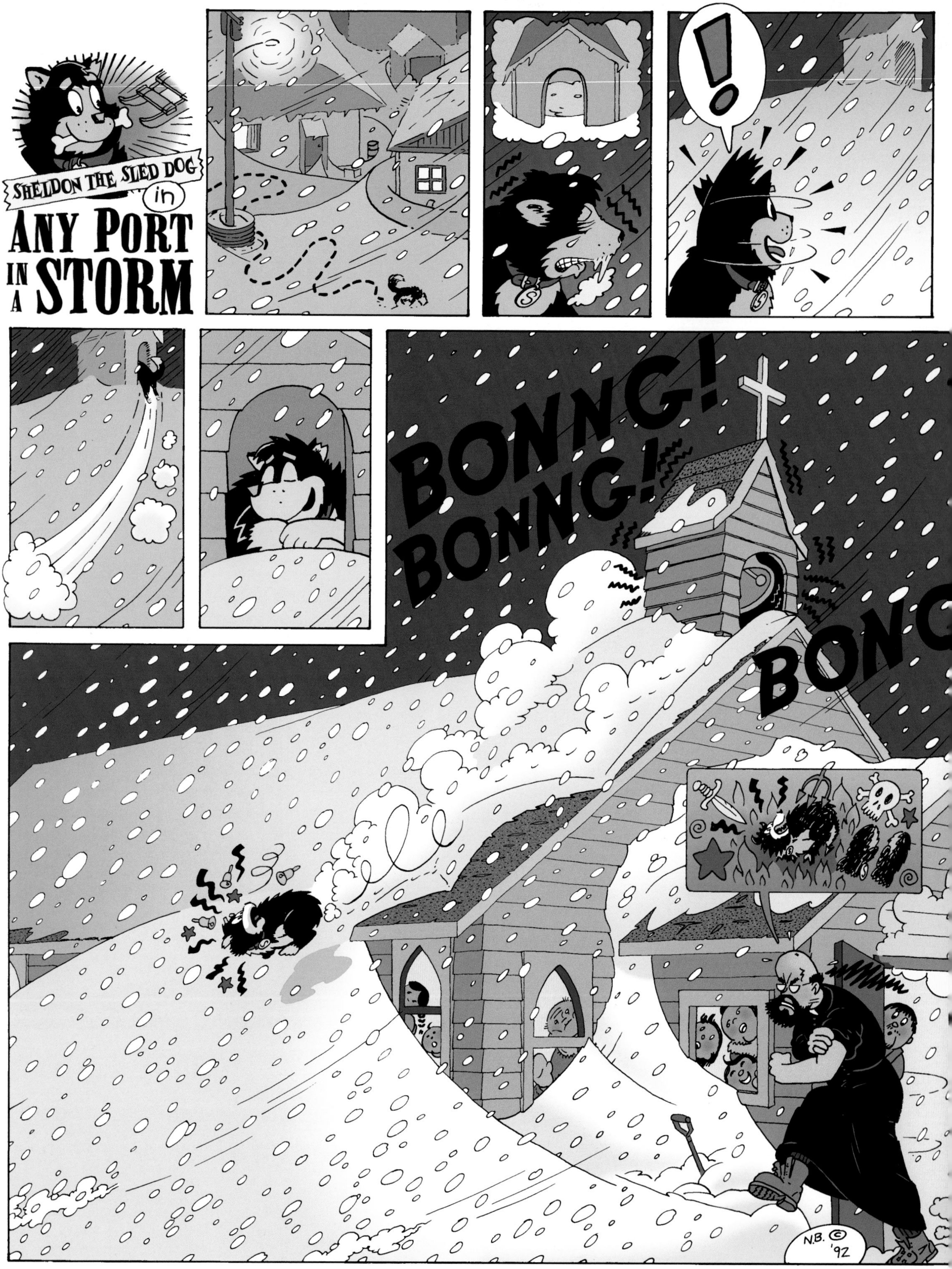
SHELDON THE SLED DOG
in
ANY PORT IN A STORM
!
BONNG!
BONNG!
BONG
N.B. © '92

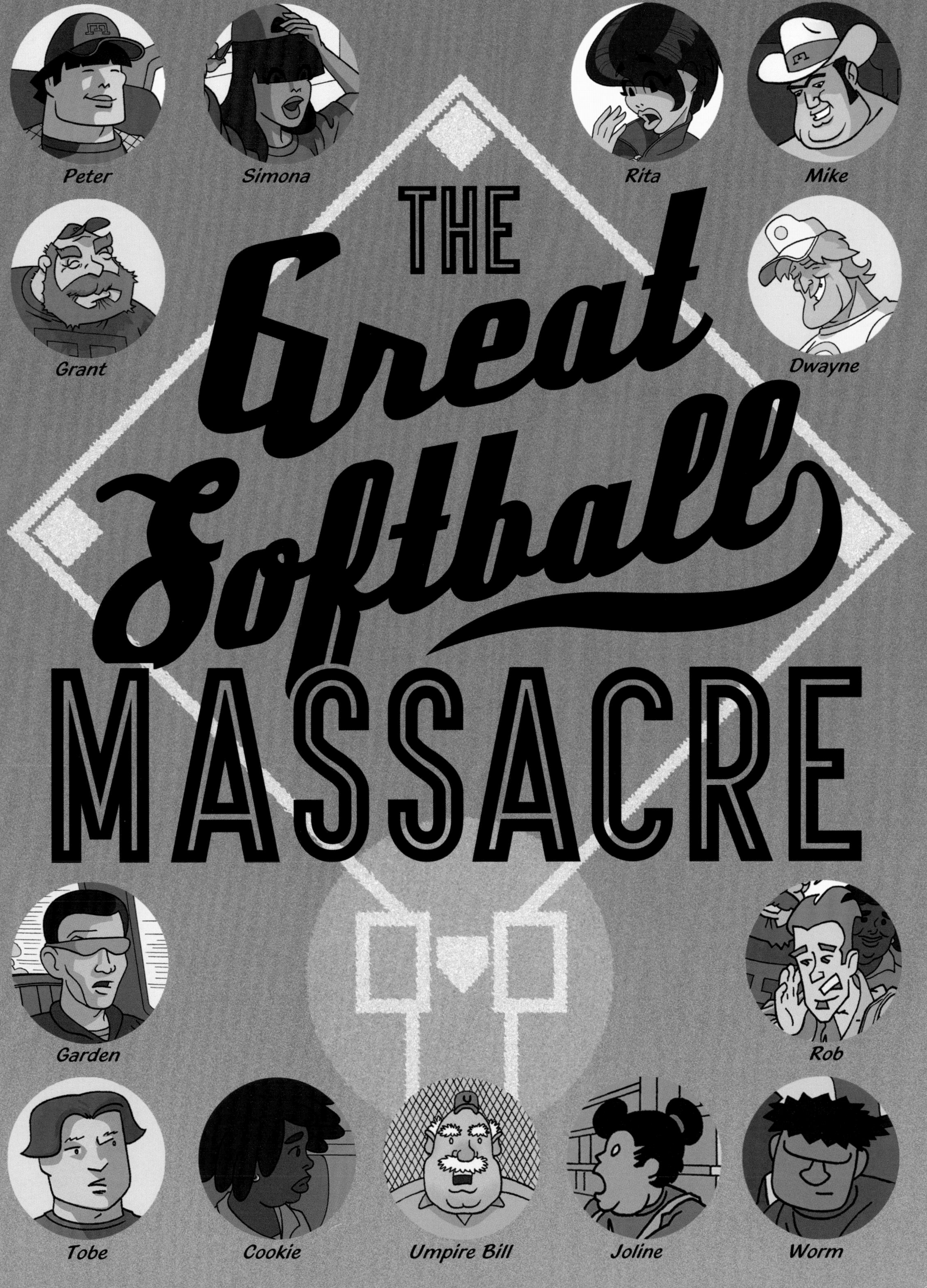
Peter
Simona
Rita
Mike
THE
Great
Softball
MASSACRE
Grant
Dwayne
Garden
Rob
Tobe
Cookie
Umpire Bill
Joline
Worm

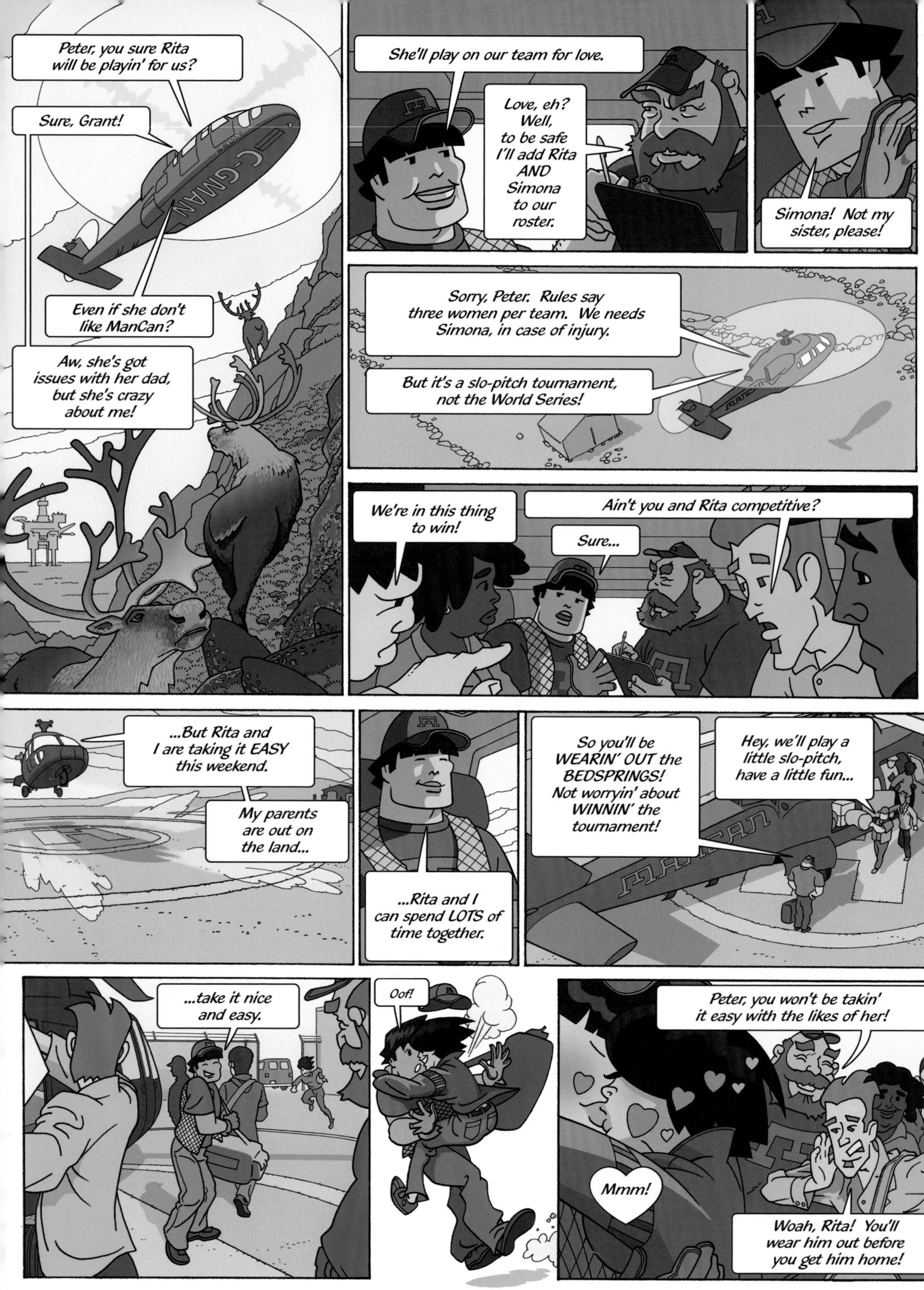
Peter, you sure Rita will be playin' for us?
Sure, Grant!
C-GMAN
Even if she don't like ManCan?
Aw, she's got issues with her dad, but she's crazy about me!
She'll play on our team for love.
Love, eh? Well, to be safe I'll add Rita AND Simona to our roster.
Simona! Not my sister, please!
Sorry, Peter. Rules say three women per team. We needs Simona, in case of injury.
But it's a slo-pitch tournament, not the World Series!
We're in this thing to win!
Ain't you and Rita competitive?
Sure...
...But Rita and I are taking it EASY this weekend.
My parents are out on the land...
...Rita and I can spend LOTS of time together.
So you'll be WEARIN' OUT the BEDSPRINGS! Not worryin' about WINNIN' the tournament!
Hey, we'll play a little slo-pitch, have a little fun...
...take it nice and easy.
Oof!
Peter, you won't be takin' it easy with the likes of her!
Mmm!
Woah, Rita! You'll wear him out before you get him home!

You ready to play ball?

More than ready!

I brought you something.

ZIIIIIP!

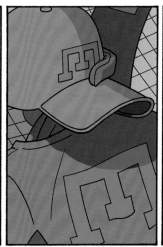

ManCan?!

I thought we were going to be on the SAME TEAM!

We are. The MANCAN team!

We can use a spare girl.

Spare?!

Your dad funds the team.

My dad?

Yeah.

Your dad runs the ManCan office, so you get to play with us.

S'right.

WRONG!

My dad may run YOUR lives, but he doesn't run MINE.

I told Peter I was working at the Harbour Lights Hotel!

And THIS is my team!

SAFE HARBOUR · HARBOUR LITES · SLO-PITCH

C'mon, Rita... you can switch teams. For me.

I CAN'T switch! I'm player and manager! YOU switch.

We've barely got enough players. These are my crewmates. My team mates!

And I'm your mate mate. Don't you want to play with me?

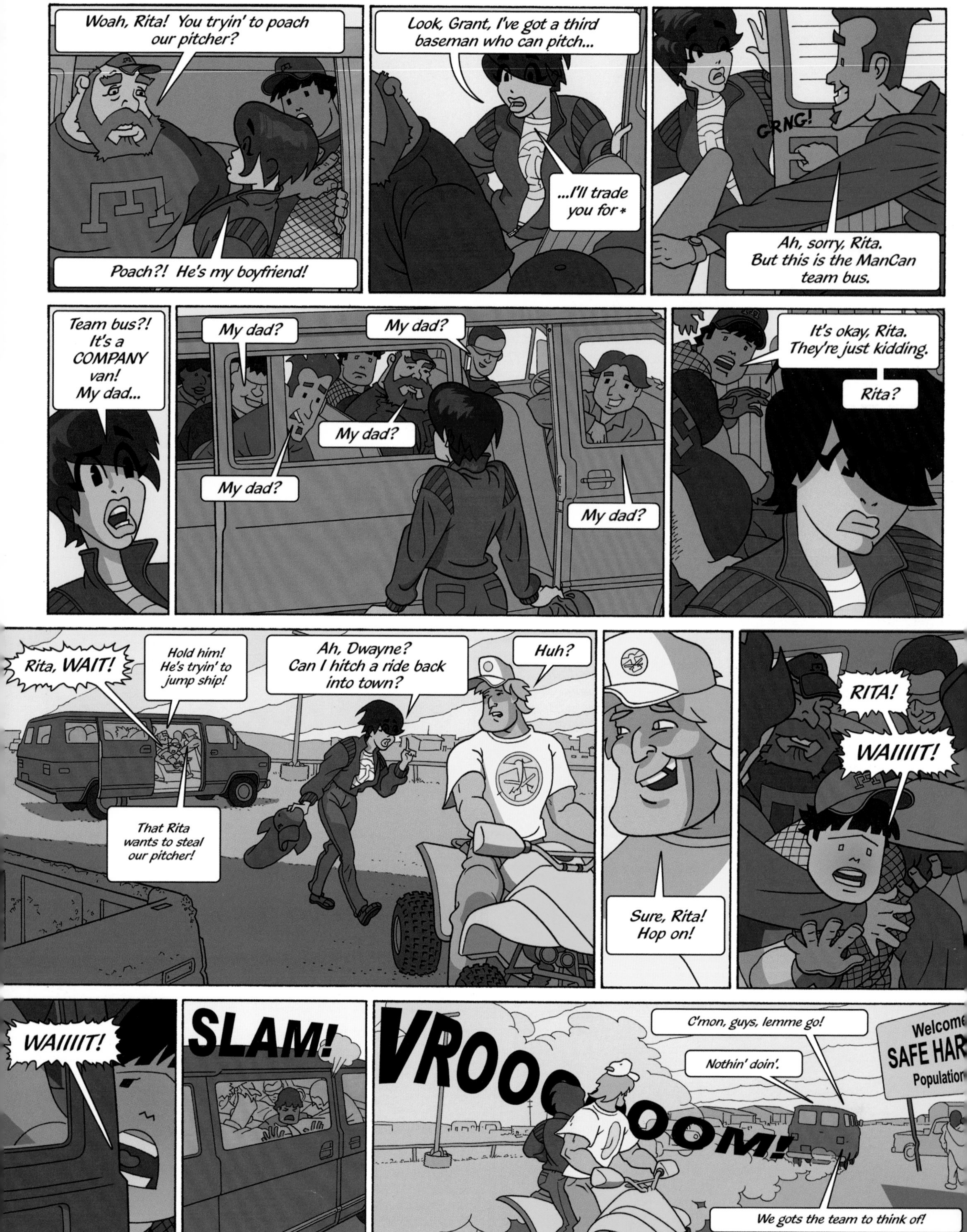

Woah, Rita! You tryin' to poach our pitcher?
Poach?! He's my boyfriend!
Look, Grant, I've got a third baseman who can pitch...
...I'll trade you for *
GRNG!
Ah, sorry, Rita. But this is the ManCan team bus.
Team bus?! It's a COMPANY van! My dad...
My dad?
My dad?
My dad?
My dad?
My dad?
It's okay, Rita. They're just kidding.
Rita?
Rita, WAIT!
Hold him! He's tryin' to jump ship!
That Rita wants to steal our pitcher!
Ah, Dwayne? Can I hitch a ride back into town?
Huh?
Sure, Rita! Hop on!
RITA!
WAIIIIT!
WAIIIIT!
SLAM!
VROOOOOOM!
C'mon, guys, lemme go!
Nothin' doin'.
We gots the team to think of!

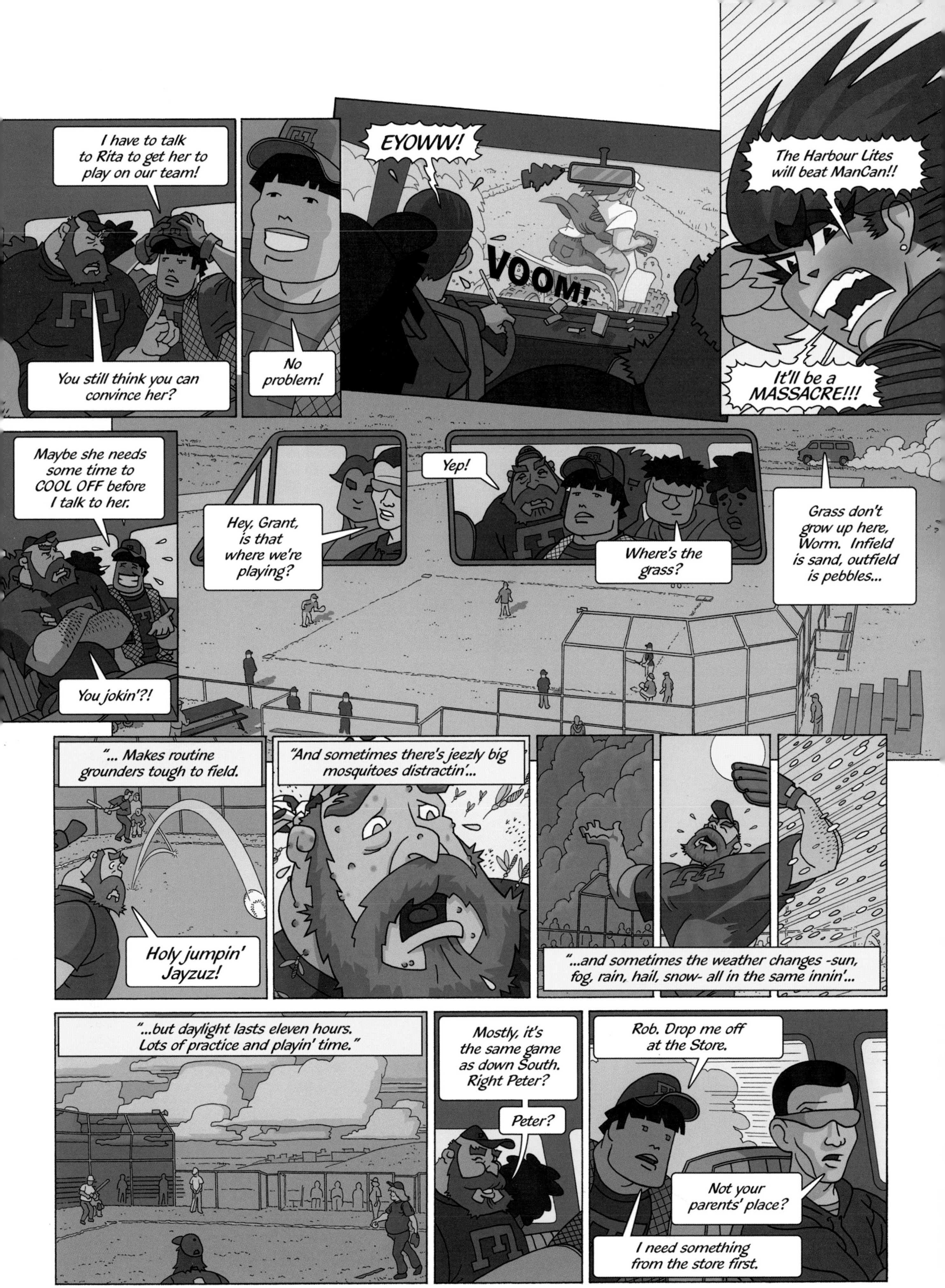
I have to talk to Rita to get her to play on our team!
You still think you can convince her?
No problem!
EYOWW!
VOOM!
The Harbour Lites will beat ManCan!!
It'll be a MASSACRE!!!
Maybe she needs some time to COOL OFF before I talk to her.
You jokin'?!
Hey, Grant, is that where we're playing?
Yep!
Where's the grass?
Grass don't grow up here, Worm. Infield is sand, outfield is pebbles...
"... Makes routine grounders tough to field.
Holy jumpin' Jayzuz!
"And sometimes there's jeezly big mosquitoes distractin'...
"...and sometimes the weather changes -sun, fog, rain, hail, snow- all in the same innin'...
"...but daylight lasts eleven hours. Lots of practice and playin' time."
Mostly, it's the same game as down South. Right Peter?
Peter?
Rob. Drop me off at the Store.
Not your parents' place?
I need something from the store first.

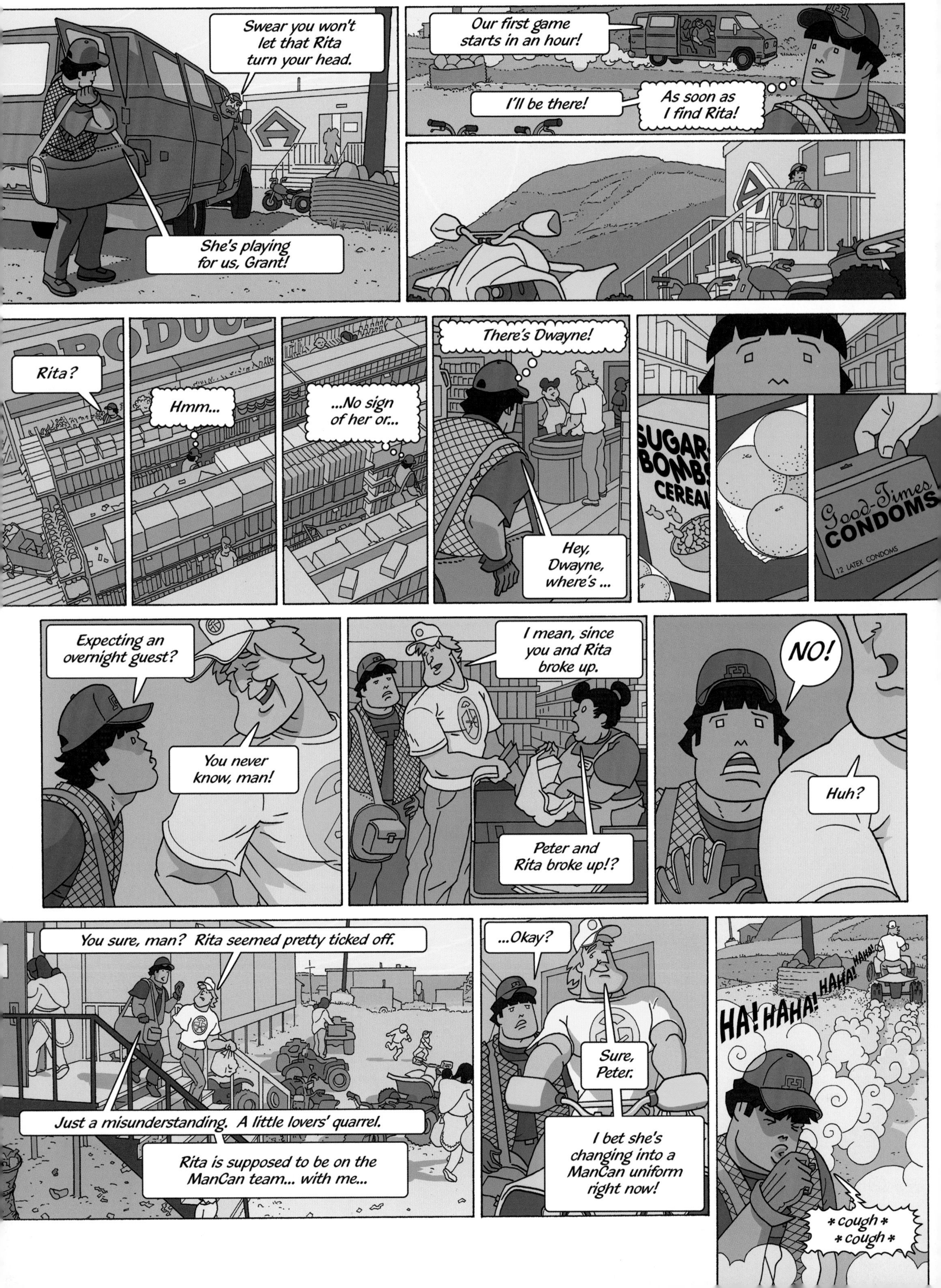
Swear you won't let that Rita turn your head.
She's playing for us, Grant!
Our first game starts in an hour!
I'll be there!
As soon as I find Rita!
Rita?
Hmm...
...No sign of her or...
There's Dwayne!
Hey, Dwayne, where's ...
SUGAR BOMBS CEREAL
Good-Times CONDOMS
12 LATEX CONDOMS
Expecting an overnight guest?
You never know, man!
I mean, since you and Rita broke up.
Peter and Rita broke up!?
NO!
Huh?
You sure, man? Rita seemed pretty ticked off.
Just a misunderstanding. A little lovers' quarrel.
Rita is supposed to be on the ManCan team... with me...
...Okay?
Sure, Peter.
I bet she's changing into a ManCan uniform right now!
HA! HAHA! HAHA! HAHA!
cough
cough

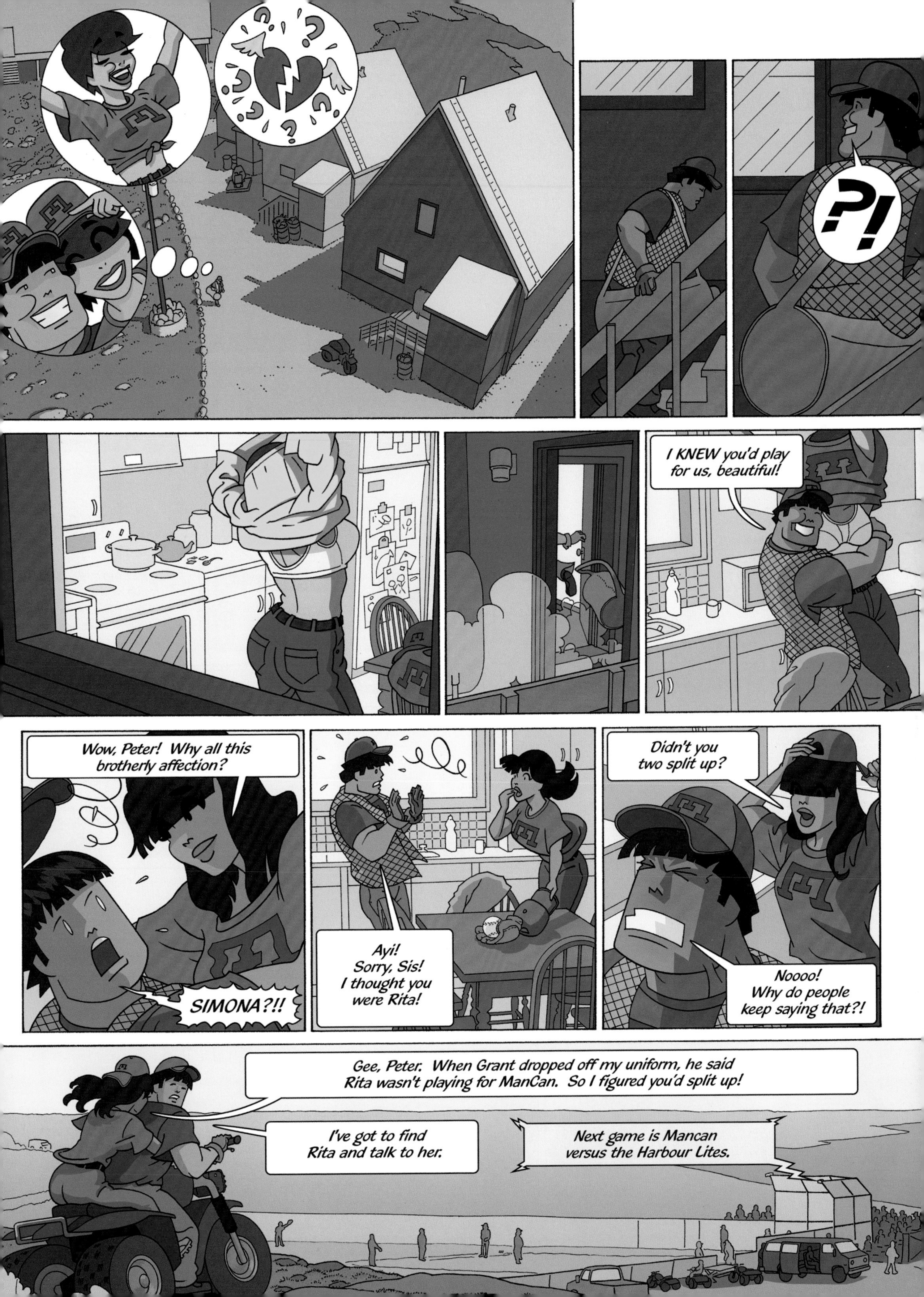
?!
I KNEW you'd play for us, beautiful!
Wow, Peter! Why all this brotherly affection?
SIMONA?!!
Ayi! Sorry, Sis! I thought you were Rita!
Didn't you two split up?
Noooo! Why do people keep saying that?!
Gee, Peter. When Grant dropped off my uniform, he said Rita wasn't playing for ManCan. So I figured you'd split up!
I've got to find Rita and talk to her.
Next game is Mancan versus the Harbour Lites.

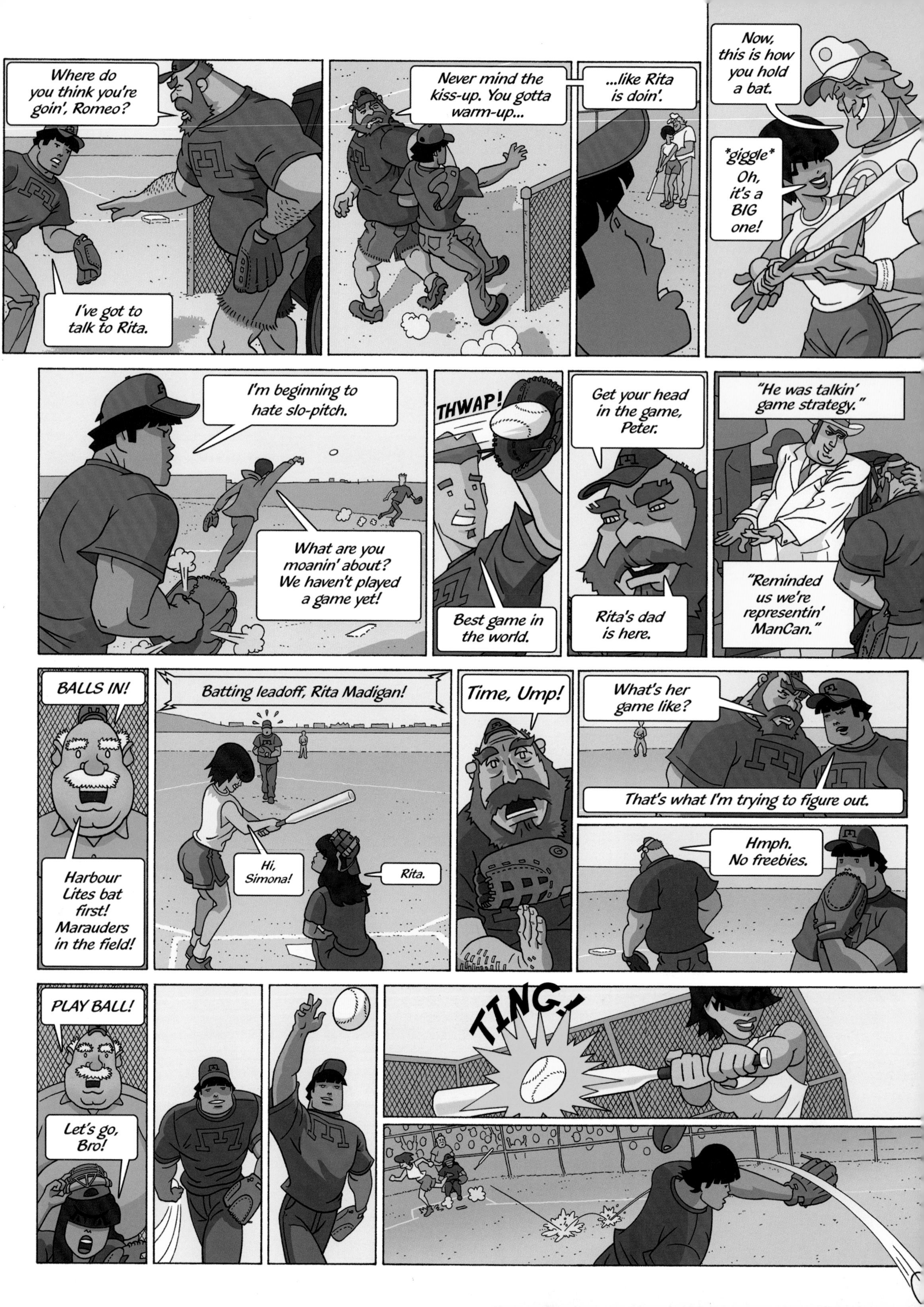

Where do you think you're goin', Romeo?
I've got to talk to Rita.
Never mind the kiss-up. You gotta warm-up...
...like Rita is doin'.
Now, this is how you hold a bat.
giggle Oh, it's a BIG one!
I'm beginning to hate slo-pitch.
What are you moanin' about? We haven't played a game yet!
THWAP!
Best game in the world.
Get your head in the game, Peter.
Rita's dad is here.
"He was talkin' game strategy."
"Reminded us we're representin' ManCan."
BALLS IN!
Harbour Lites bat first! Marauders in the field!
Batting leadoff, Rita Madigan!
Hi, Simona!
Rita.
Time, Ump!
What's her game like?
That's what I'm trying to figure out.
Hmph. No freebies.
PLAY BALL!
Let's go, Bro!
TING!

WAP!

SAFE AT FIRST!

Not a lot of power, but she can really place the ball.

Knows how to hurt you.

Oh yeah.

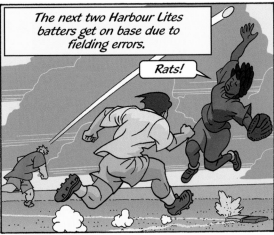

The next two Harbour Lites batters get on base due to fielding errors.

Rats!

Son of a birchbark biscuit box!

Rita advances to third.

Rita, I *

C'mon Dwayne, hit me home!

Uh-oh.

Back up! He's got power.

C'mon Dwayne! Pound it out of here!

Go Lites!

GO!

GO!

Go MANCAN!

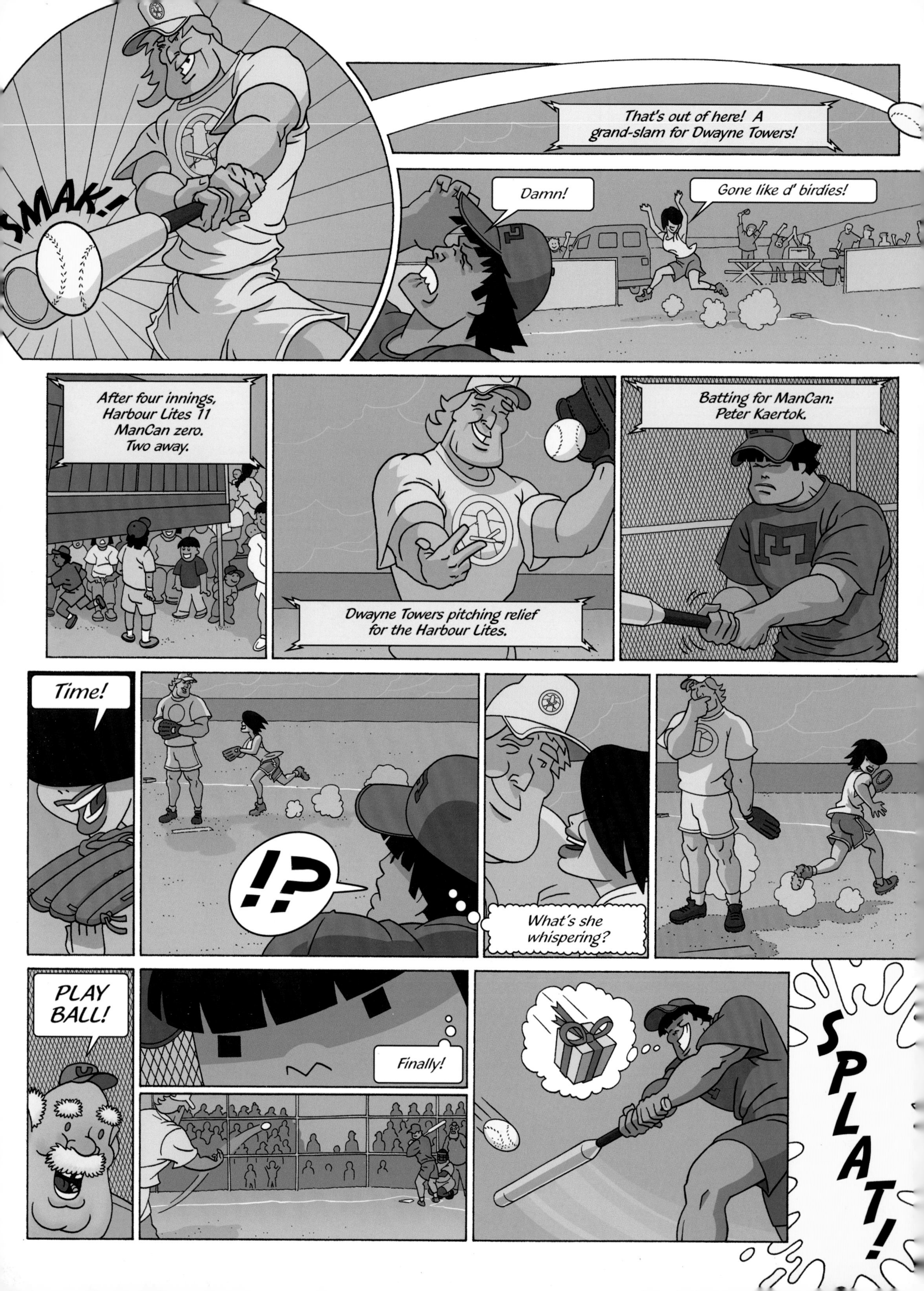
SMAK!
That's out of here! A grand-slam for Dwayne Towers!
Damn!
Gone like d' birdies!
After four innings, Harbour Lites 11 ManCan zero. Two away.
Dwayne Towers pitching relief for the Harbour Lites.
Batting for ManCan: Peter Kaertok.
Time!
!?
What's she whispering?
PLAY BALL!
Finally!
SPLAT!

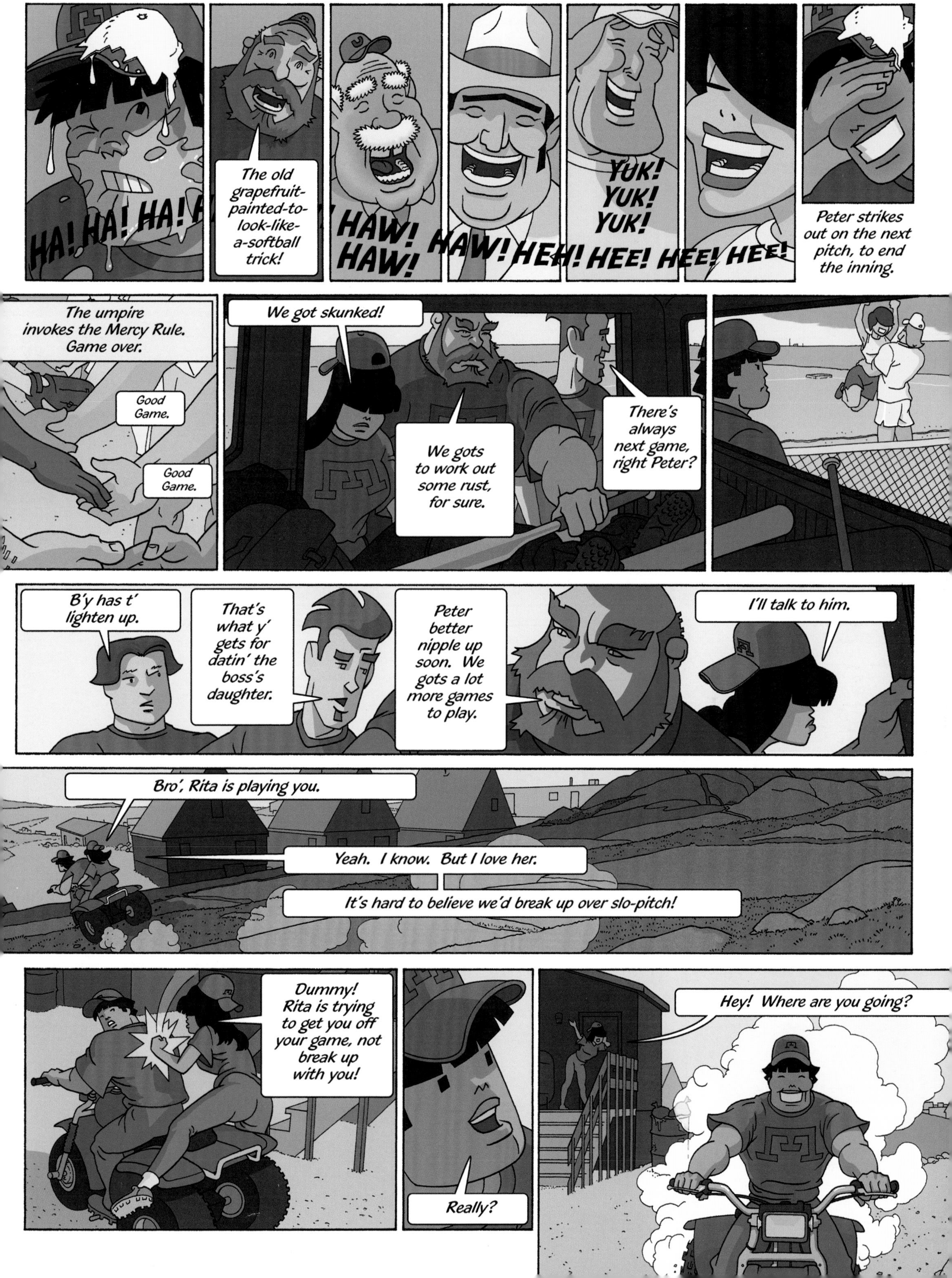
HA! HA! HA! HA!
The old grapefruit-painted-to-look-like-a-softball trick!
HAW! HAW!
HAW!
HEH!
YUK! YUK! YUK!
HEE! HEE! HEE!
Peter strikes out on the next pitch, to end the inning.
The umpire invokes the Mercy Rule. Game over.
Good Game.
Good Game.
We got skunked!
We gots to work out some rust, for sure.
There's always next game, right Peter?
B'y has t' lighten up.
That's what y' gets for datin' the boss's daughter.
Peter better nipple up soon. We gots a lot more games to play.
I'll talk to him.
Bro', Rita is playing you.
Yeah. I know. But I love her.
It's hard to believe we'd break up over slo-pitch!
Dummy! Rita is trying to get you off your game, not break up with you!
Really?
Hey! Where are you going?

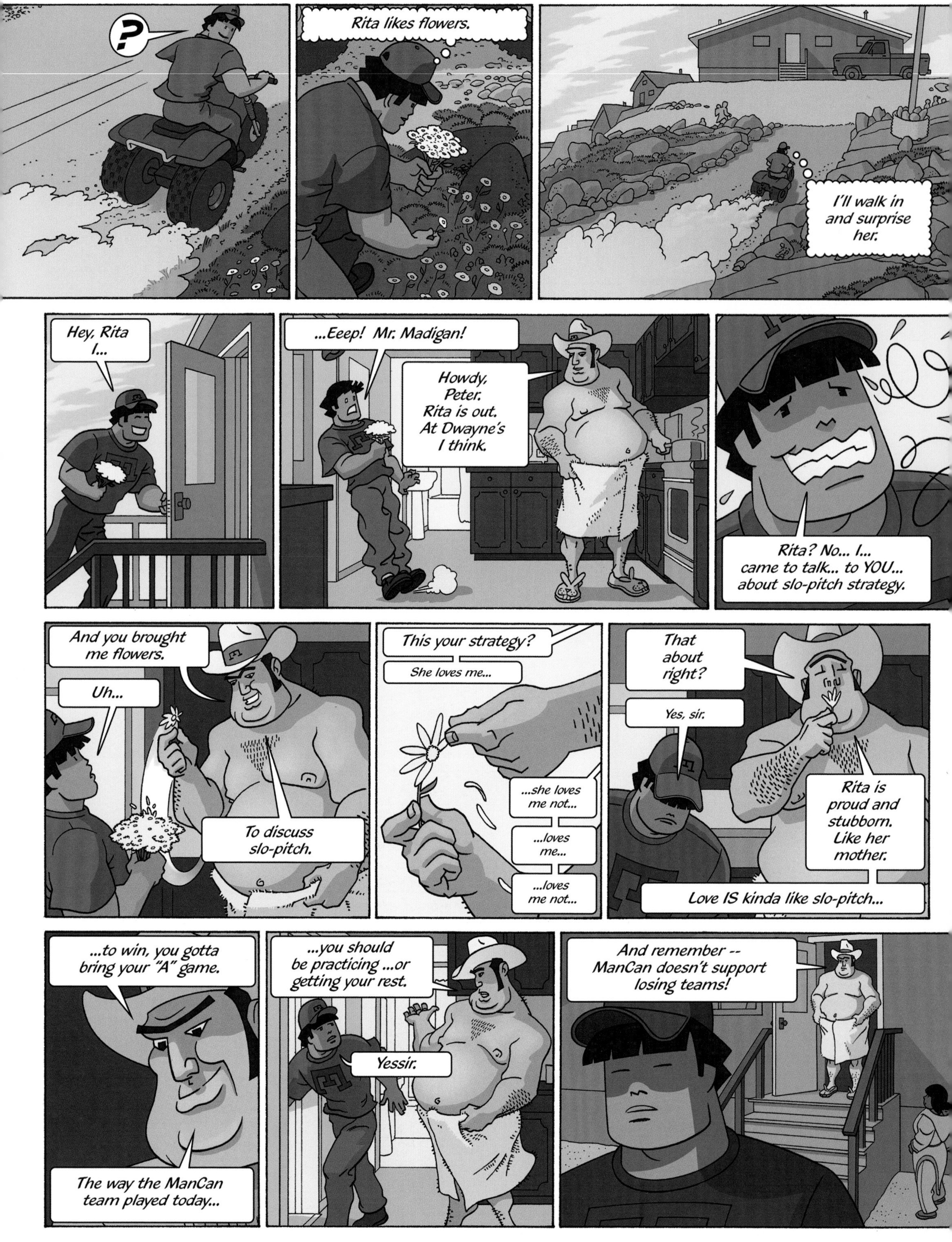
?
Rita likes flowers.
I'll walk in and surprise her.
Hey, Rita I...
...Eeep! Mr. Madigan!
Howdy, Peter. Rita is out. At Dwayne's I think.
Rita? No... I... came to talk... to YOU... about slo-pitch strategy.
And you brought me flowers.
Uh...
To discuss slo-pitch.
This your strategy?
She loves me...
...she loves me not...
...loves me...
...loves me not...
That about right?
Yes, sir.
Rita is proud and stubborn. Like her mother.
Love IS kinda like slo-pitch...
...to win, you gotta bring your "A" game.
The way the ManCan team played today...
...you should be practicing ...or getting your rest.
Yessir.
And remember -- ManCan doesn't support losing teams!

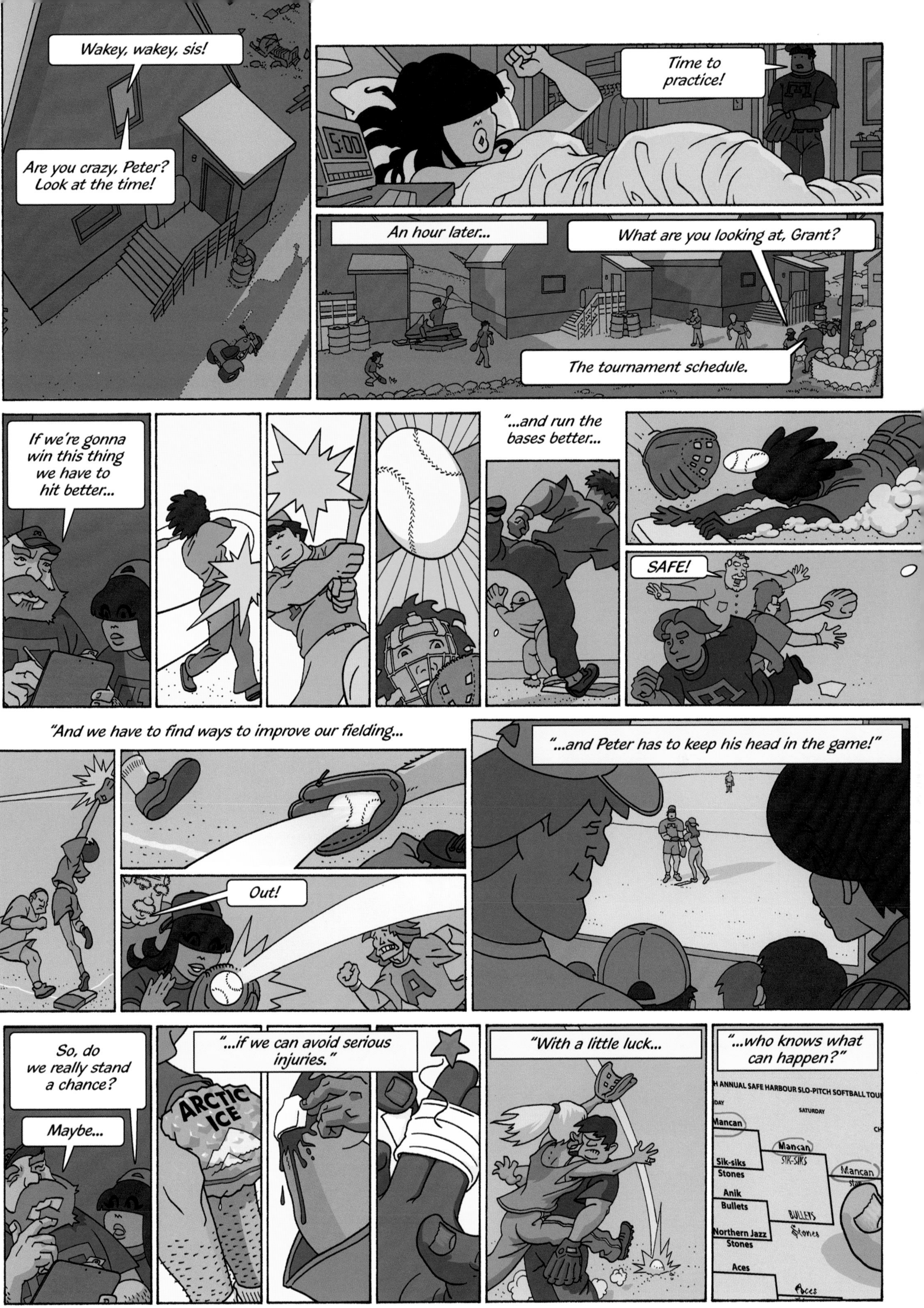
Wakey, wakey, sis!
Are you crazy, Peter? Look at the time!
5:00
Time to practice!
An hour later...
What are you looking at, Grant?
The tournament schedule.
If we're gonna win this thing we have to hit better...
"...and run the bases better...
SAFE!
"And we have to find ways to improve our fielding...
Out!
"...and Peter has to keep his head in the game!"
So, do we really stand a chance?
Maybe...
"...if we can avoid serious injuries."
ARCTIC ICE
"With a little luck...
"...who knows what can happen?"
H ANNUAL SAFE HARBOUR SLO-PITCH SOFTBALL TOU
DAY
SATURDAY
CH
Mancan
Sik-siks
Stones
Anik
Bullets
Northern Jazz
Stones
Aces
Mancan
SIK-SIKS
BULLETS
Stones
Aces
Mancan

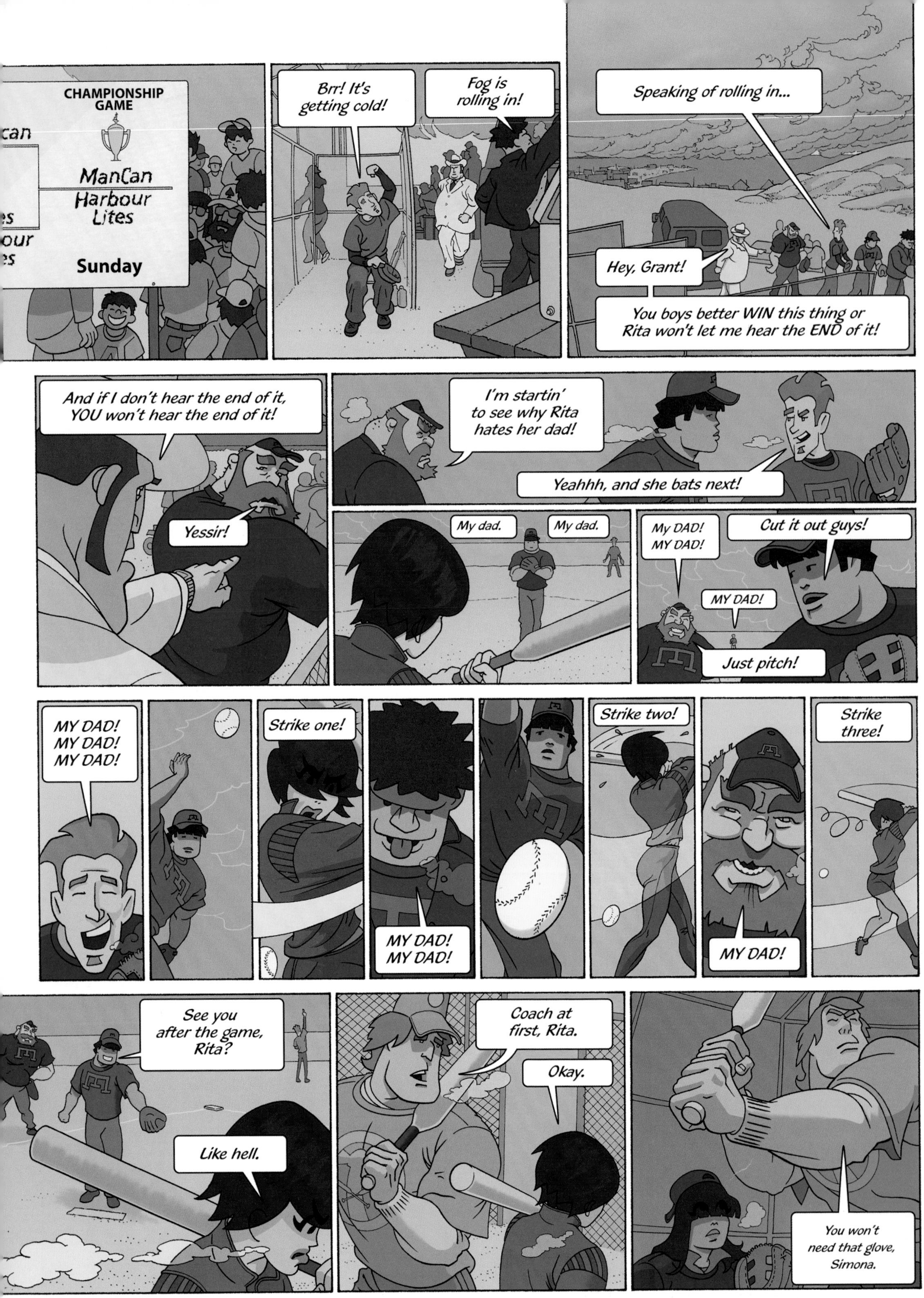
CHAMPIONSHIP GAME
ManCan
Harbour Lites
Sunday
Brr! It's getting cold!
Fog is rolling in!
Speaking of rolling in...
Hey, Grant!
You boys better WIN this thing or Rita won't let me hear the END of it!
And if I don't hear the end of it, YOU won't hear the end of it!
Yessir!
I'm startin' to see why Rita hates her dad!
Yeahhh, and she bats next!
My dad.
My dad.
My DAD! MY DAD!
Cut it out guys!
MY DAD!
Just pitch!
MY DAD! MY DAD! MY DAD!
Strike one!
MY DAD! MY DAD!
Strike two!
MY DAD!
Strike three!
See you after the game, Rita?
Like hell.
Coach at first, Rita.
Okay.
You won't need that glove, Simona.

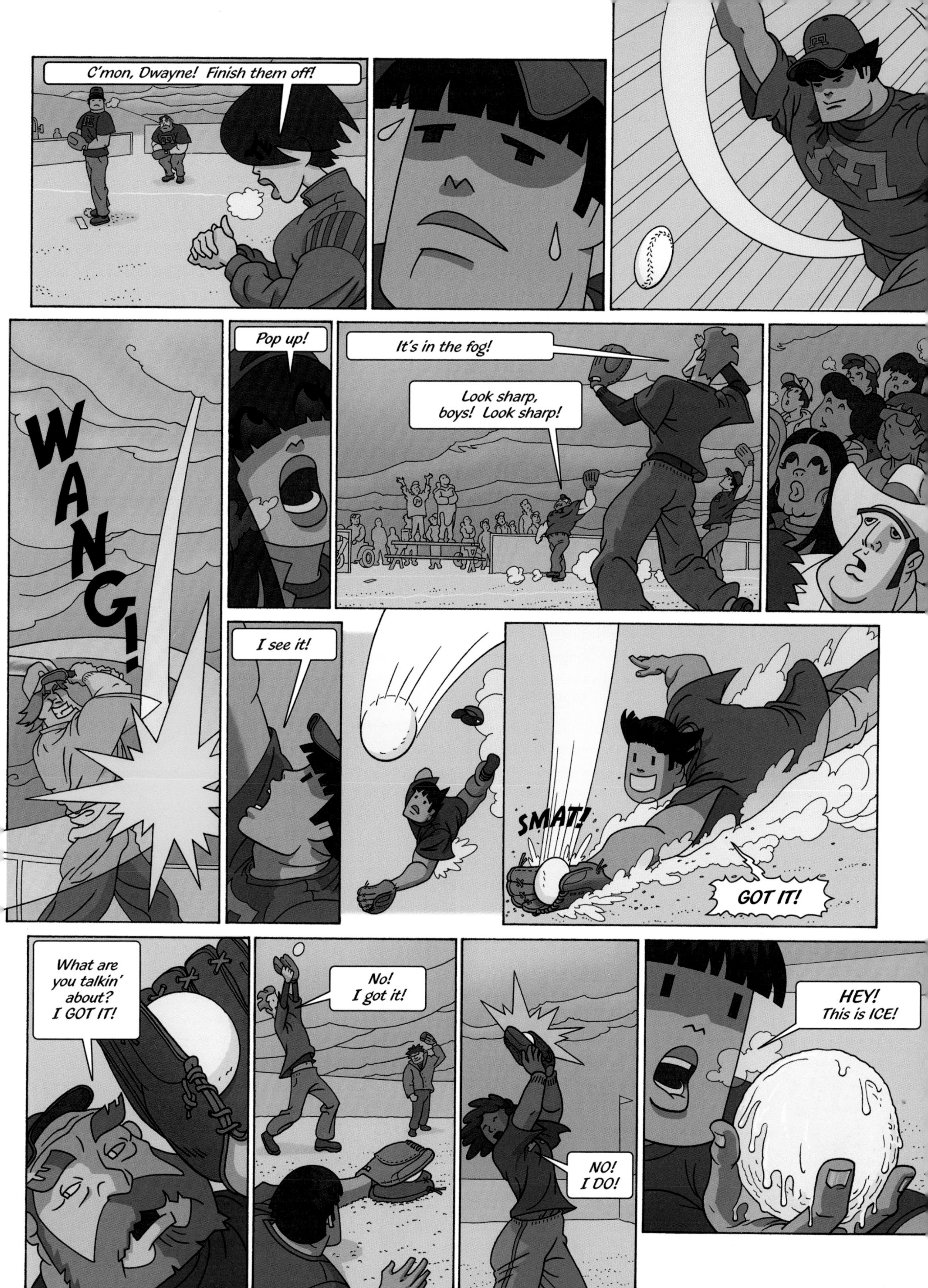
C'mon, Dwayne! Finish them off!
WANG!
Pop up!
It's in the fog!
Look sharp, boys! Look sharp!
I see it!
SMAT!
GOT IT!
What are you talkin' about? I GOT IT!
No! I got it!
NO! I DO!
HEY! This is ICE!

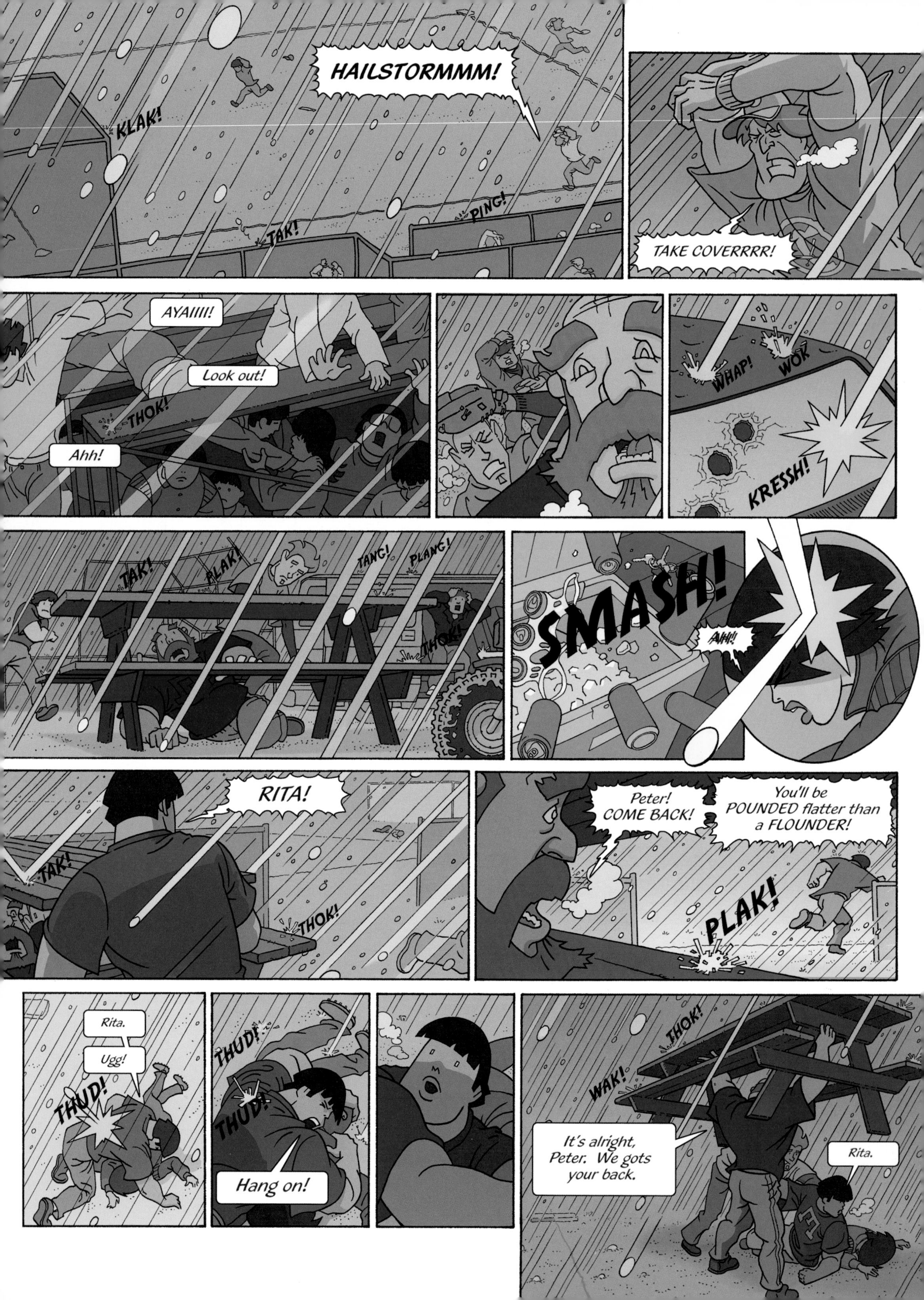
HAILSTORMMM!
KLAK!
TAK!
PING!
TAKE COVERRRR!
AYAIIII!
Look out!
THOK!
Ahh!
WHAP!
WOK
KRESSH!
TAK!
PLAK!
TANG!
PLANG!
THOK!
SMASH!
AHH!
RITA!
TAK!
THOK!
Peter! COME BACK!
You'll be POUNDED flatter than a FLOUNDER!
PLAK!
Rita.
Ugg!
THUD!
THUD!
THUD!
Hang on!
THOK!
WAK!
It's alright, Peter. We gots your back.
Rita.

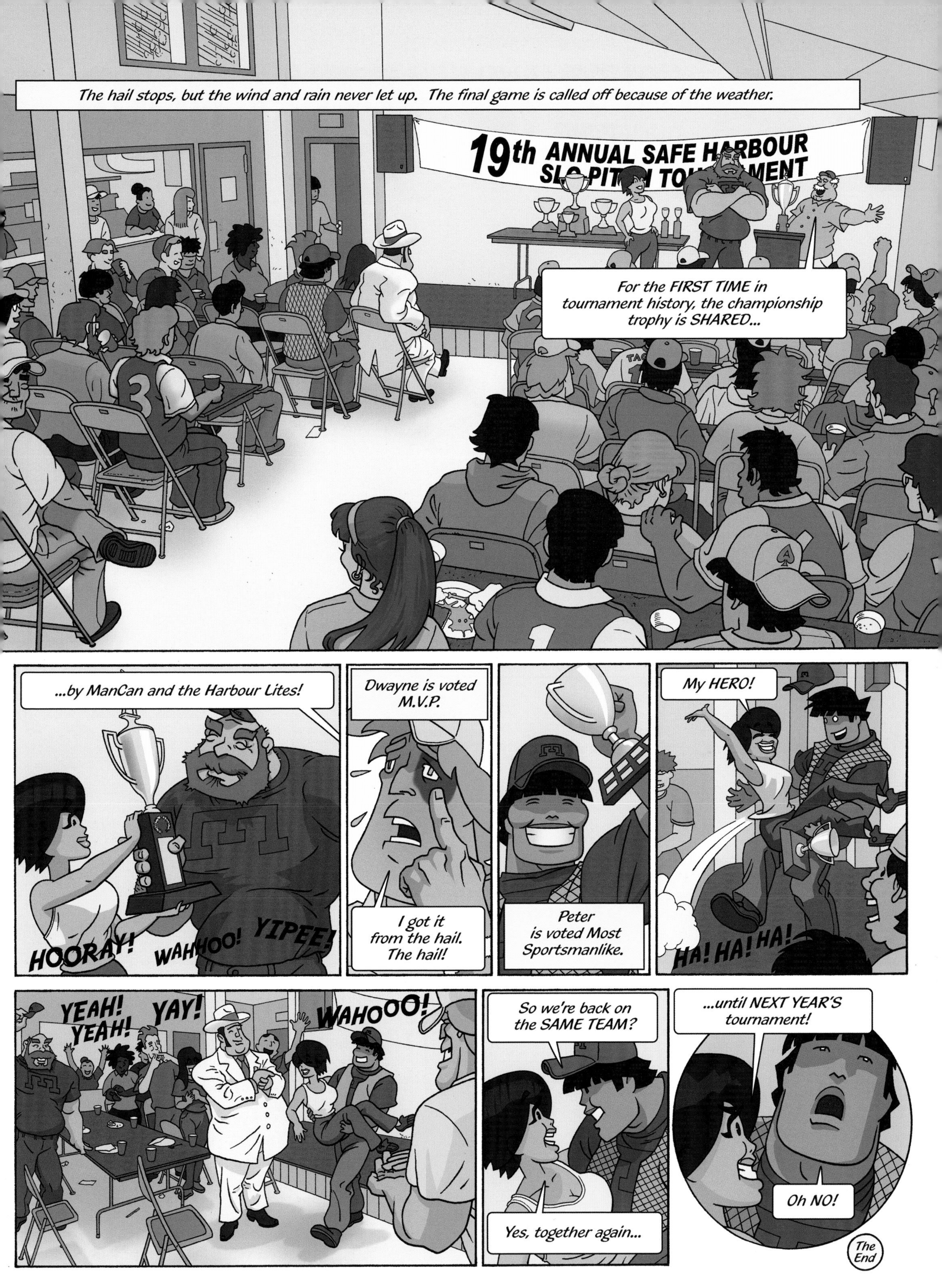
The hail stops, but the wind and rain never let up. The final game is called off because of the weather.
19th ANNUAL SAFE HARBOUR SLO PITCH TOURNAMENT
For the FIRST TIME in tournament history, the championship trophy is SHARED...
...by ManCan and the Harbour Lites!
HOORAY! WAHHOO! YIPEE!
Dwayne is voted M.V.P.
I got it from the hail. The hail!
Peter is voted Most Sportsmanlike.
My HERO!
HA! HA! HA!
YEAH! YEAH! YAY!
WAHOOO!
So we're back on the SAME TEAM?
Yes, together again...
...until NEXT YEAR'S tournament!
Oh NO!
The End

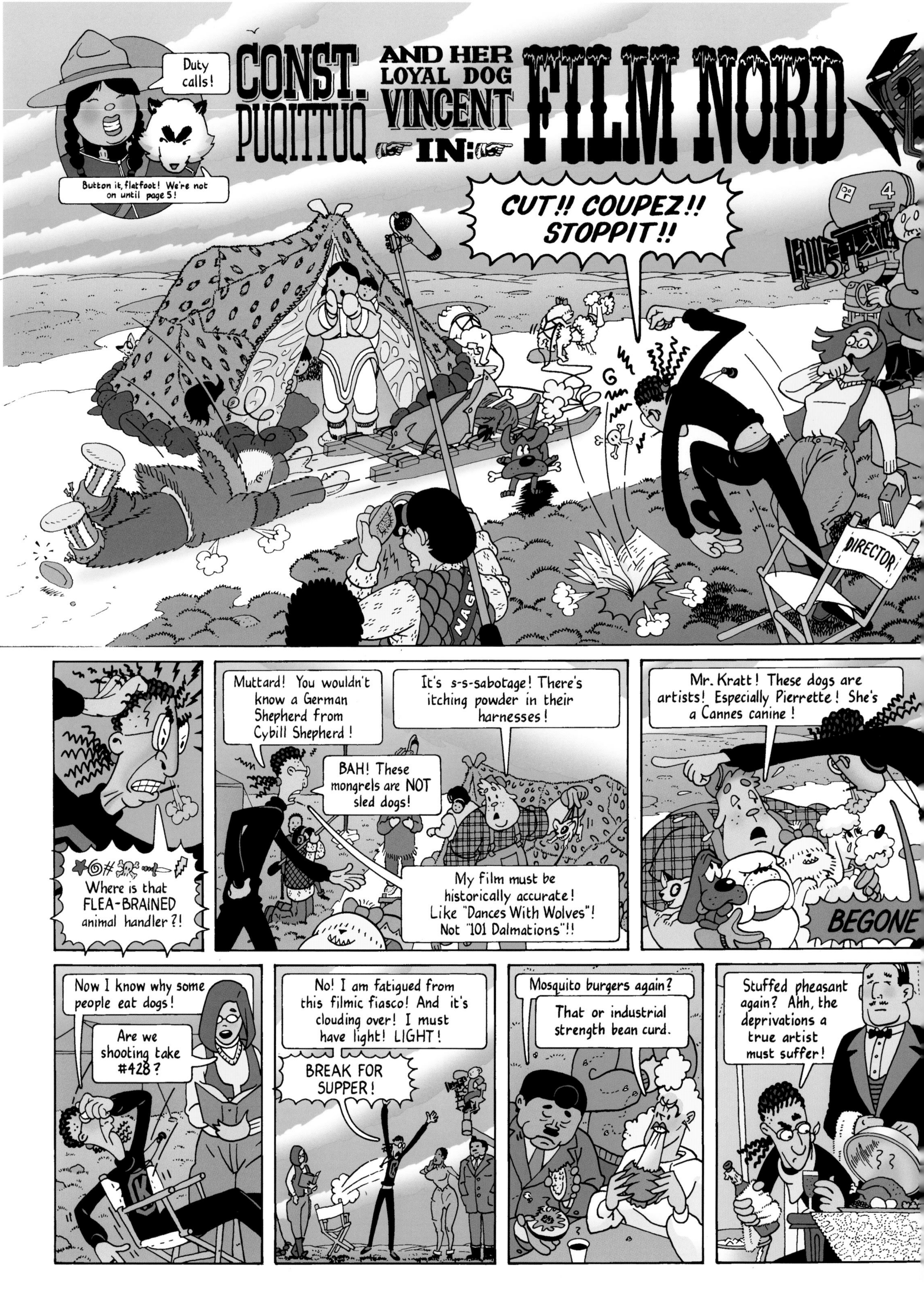
CONST. PUQITTUQ AND HER LOYAL DOG VINCENT IN: FILM NORD
Duty calls!
Button it, flatfoot! We're not on until page 5!
CUT!! COUPEZ!! STOPPIT!!
DIRECTOR
*@#☠ Where is that FLEA-BRAINED animal handler?!
Muttard! You wouldn't know a German Shepherd from Cybill Shepherd!
It's s-s-sabotage! There's itching powder in their harnesses!
BAH! These mongrels are NOT sled dogs!
My film must be historically accurate! Like "Dances With Wolves"! Not "101 Dalmations"!!
Mr. Kratt! These dogs are artists! Especially Pierrette! She's a Cannes canine!
BEGONE
Now I know why some people eat dogs!
Are we shooting take #428?
No! I am fatigued from this filmic fiasco! And it's clouding over! I must have light! LIGHT!
BREAK FOR SUPPER!
Mosquito burgers again?
That or industrial strength bean curd.
Stuffed pheasant again? Ahh, the deprivations a true artist must suffer!

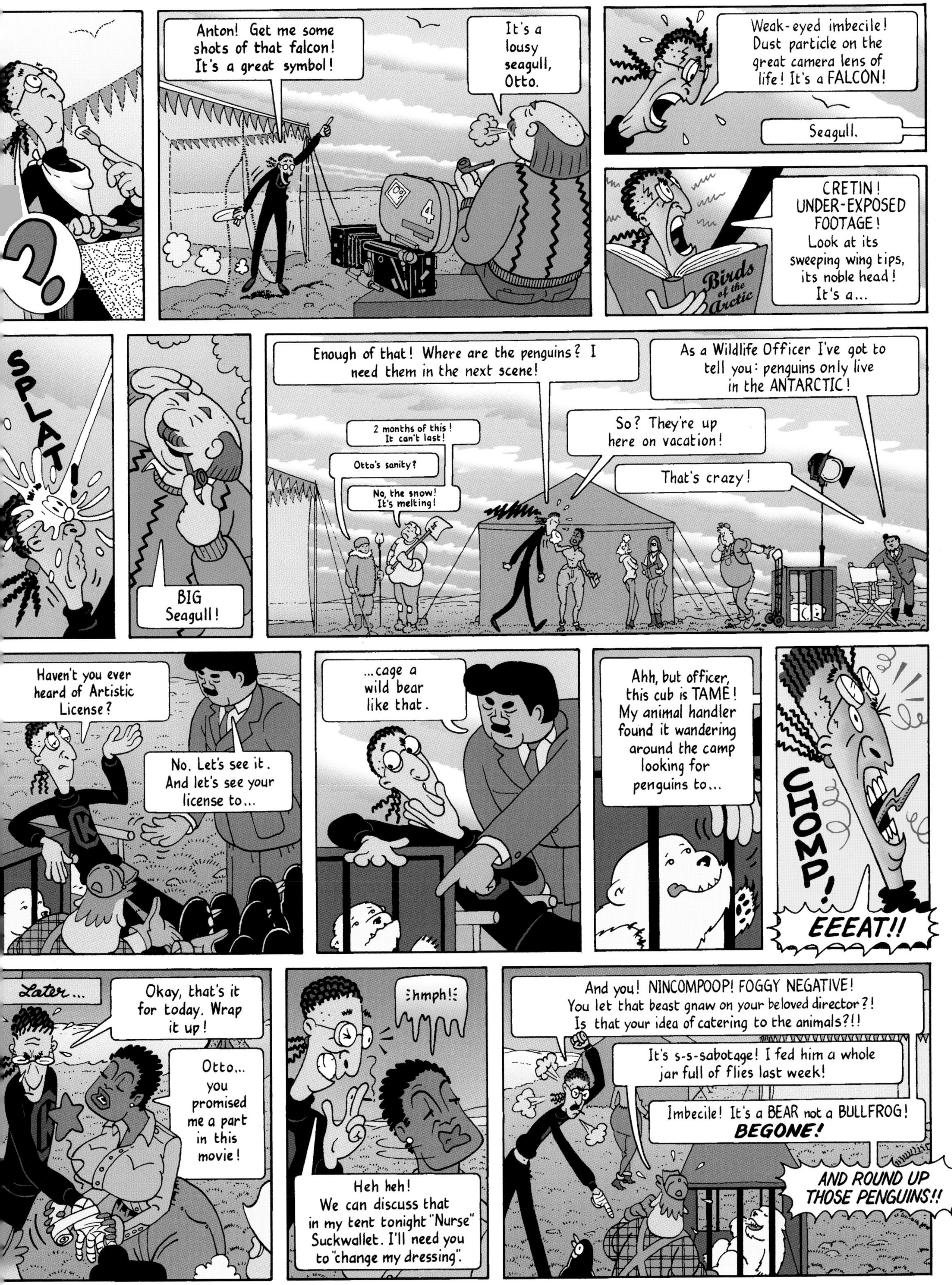
Anton! Get me some shots of that falcon! It's a great symbol!
It's a lousy seagull, Otto.
Weak-eyed imbecile! Dust particle on the great camera lens of life! It's a FALCON!
Seagull.
CRETIN! UNDER-EXPOSED FOOTAGE! Look at its sweeping wing tips, its noble head! It's a...
Birds of the Arctic
SPLAT!
BIG Seagull!
Enough of that! Where are the penguins? I need them in the next scene!
As a Wildlife Officer I've got to tell you: penguins only live in the ANTARCTIC!
So? They're up here on vacation!
That's crazy!
2 months of this! It can't last!
Otto's sanity?
No, the snow! It's melting!
Haven't you ever heard of Artistic License?
No. Let's see it. And let's see your license to...
...cage a wild bear like that.
Ahh, but officer, this cub is TAME! My animal handler found it wandering around the camp looking for penguins to...
CHOMP!
EEEAT!!
Later...
Okay, that's it for today. Wrap it up!
Otto... you promised me a part in this movie!
hmph!
Heh heh! We can discuss that in my tent tonight "Nurse" Suckwallet. I'll need you to "change my dressing".
And you! NINCOMPOOP! FOGGY NEGATIVE! You let that beast gnaw on your beloved director?! Is that your idea of catering to the animals?!!
It's s-s-sabotage! I fed him a whole jar full of flies last week!
Imbecile! It's a BEAR not a BULLFROG! BEGONE!
AND ROUND UP THOSE PENGUINS!!

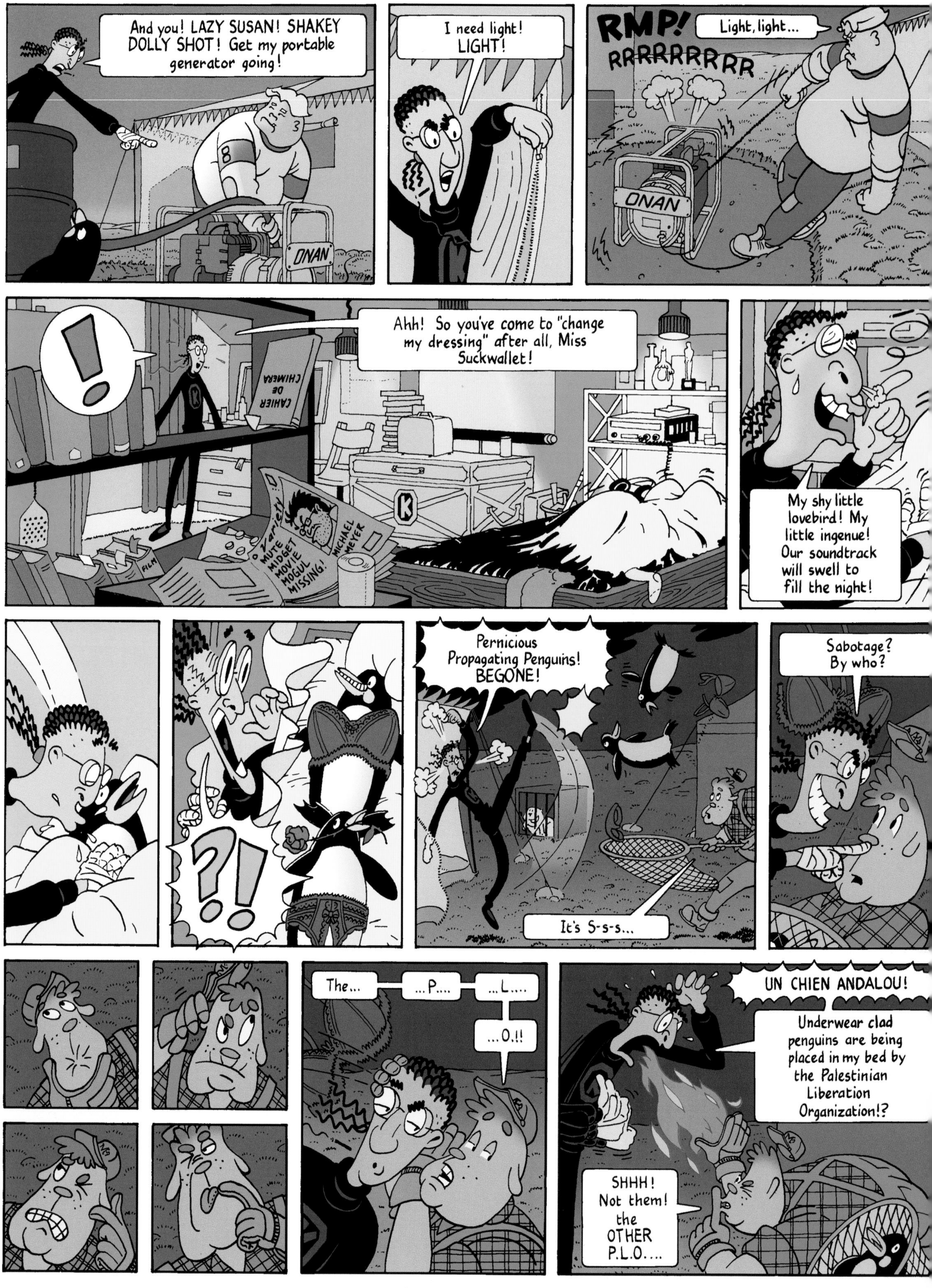

And you! LAZY SUSAN! SHAKEY DOLLY SHOT! Get my portable generator going!
ONAN
I need light! LIGHT!
RMP!
Light, light...
RRRRRRRRR
ONAN
!
Ahh! So you've come to "change my dressing" after all, Miss Suckwallet!
CAHIER DE CHIMERA
Variety
MUTE MIDGET MOVIE MOGUL MISSING!
MICHAEL MEYER
FILM
My shy little lovebird! My little ingenue! Our soundtrack will swell to fill the night!
?!
Pernicious Propagating Penguins! BEGONE!
It's S-s-s...
Sabotage? By who?
The...
...P....
...L....
...O.!!
UN CHIEN ANDALOU!
Underwear clad penguins are being placed in my bed by the Palestinian Liberation Organization!?
SHHH! Not them! the OTHER P.L.O....

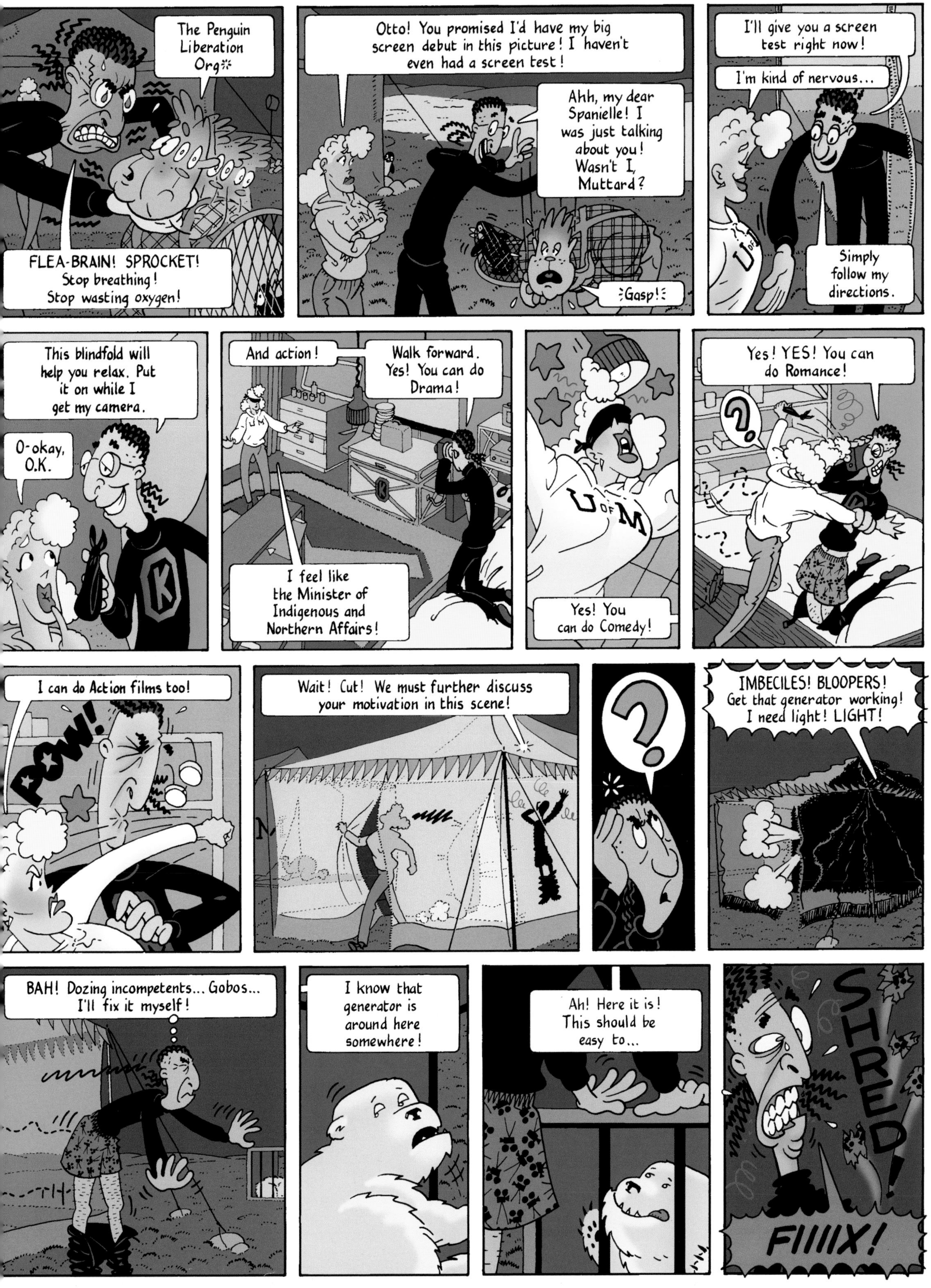

The Penguin Liberation Org☼
FLEA-BRAIN! SPROCKET! Stop breathing! Stop wasting oxygen!
Otto! You promised I'd have my big screen debut in this picture! I haven't even had a screen test!
Ahh, my dear Spanielle! I was just talking about you! Wasn't I, Muttard?
Gasp!
I'll give you a screen test right now!
I'm kind of nervous...
Simply follow my directions.
This blindfold will help you relax. Put it on while I get my camera.
O-okay, O.K.
And action!
Walk forward. Yes! You can do Drama!
I feel like the Minister of Indigenous and Northern Affairs!
Yes! You can do Comedy!
Yes! YES! You can do Romance!
I can do Action films too!
POW!
Wait! Cut! We must further discuss your motivation in this scene!
IMBECILES! BLOOPERS! Get that generator working! I need light! LIGHT!
BAH! Dozing incompetents... Gobos... I'll fix it myself!
I know that generator is around here somewhere!
Ah! Here it is! This should be easy to...
SHRED!
FIIIIX!

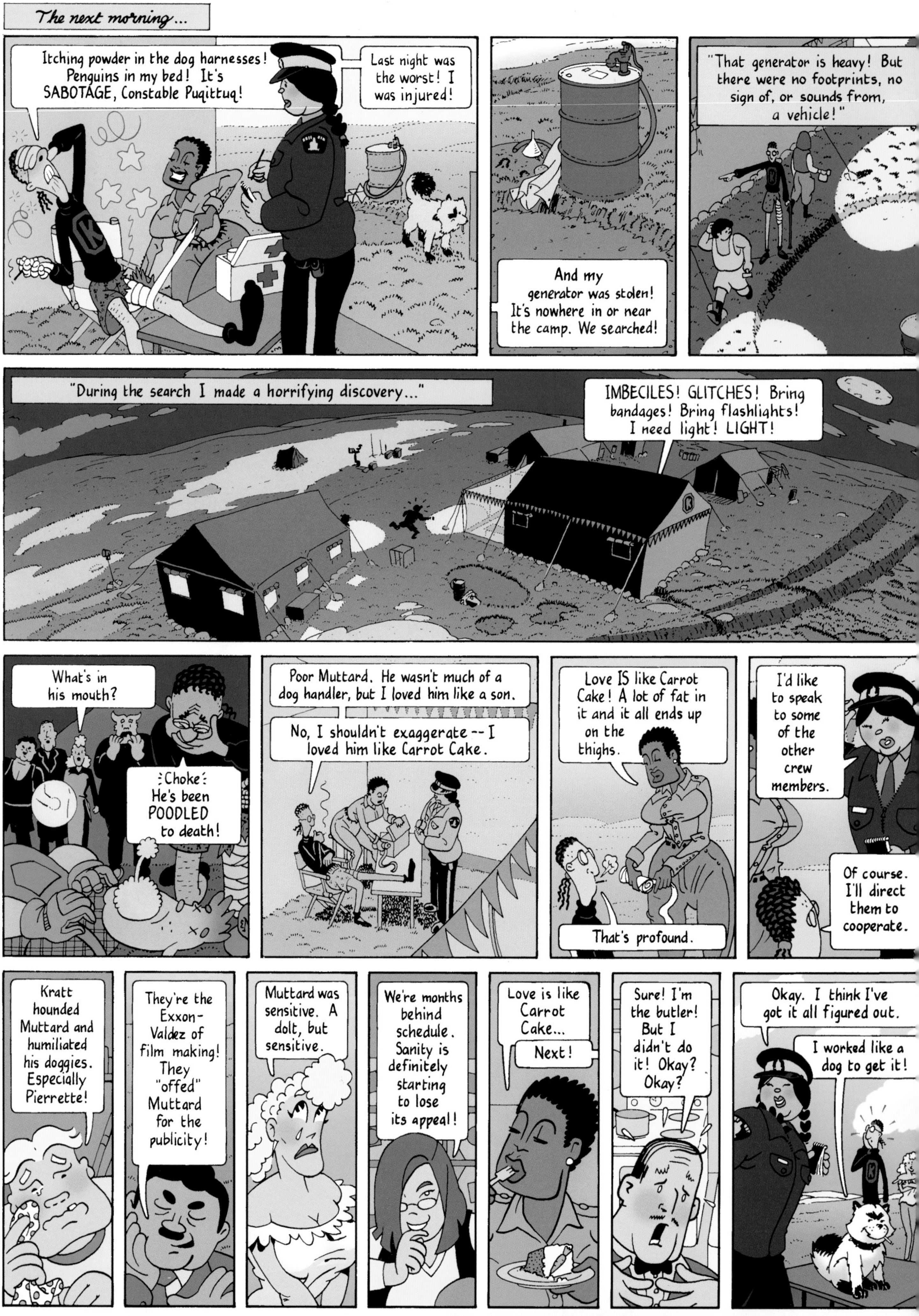
The next morning...
Itching powder in the dog harnesses! Penguins in my bed! It's SABOTAGE, Constable Puqittuq!
Last night was the worst! I was injured!
And my generator was stolen! It's nowhere in or near the camp. We searched!
"That generator is heavy! But there were no footprints, no sign of, or sounds from, a vehicle!"
"During the search I made a horrifying discovery..."
IMBECILES! GLITCHES! Bring bandages! Bring flashlights! I need light! LIGHT!
What's in his mouth?
:Choke: He's been POODLED to death!
Poor Muttard. He wasn't much of a dog handler, but I loved him like a son.
No, I shouldn't exaggerate -- I loved him like Carrot Cake.
Love IS like Carrot Cake! A lot of fat in it and it all ends up on the thighs.
That's profound.
I'd like to speak to some of the other crew members.
Of course. I'll direct them to cooperate.
Kratt hounded Muttard and humiliated his doggies. Especially Pierrette!
They're the Exxon-Valdez of film making! They "offed" Muttard for the publicity!
Muttard was sensitive. A dolt, but sensitive.
We're months behind schedule. Sanity is definitely starting to lose its appeal!
Love is like Carrot Cake...
Next!
Sure! I'm the butler! But I didn't do it! Okay? Okay?
Okay. I think I've got it all figured out.
I worked like a dog to get it!

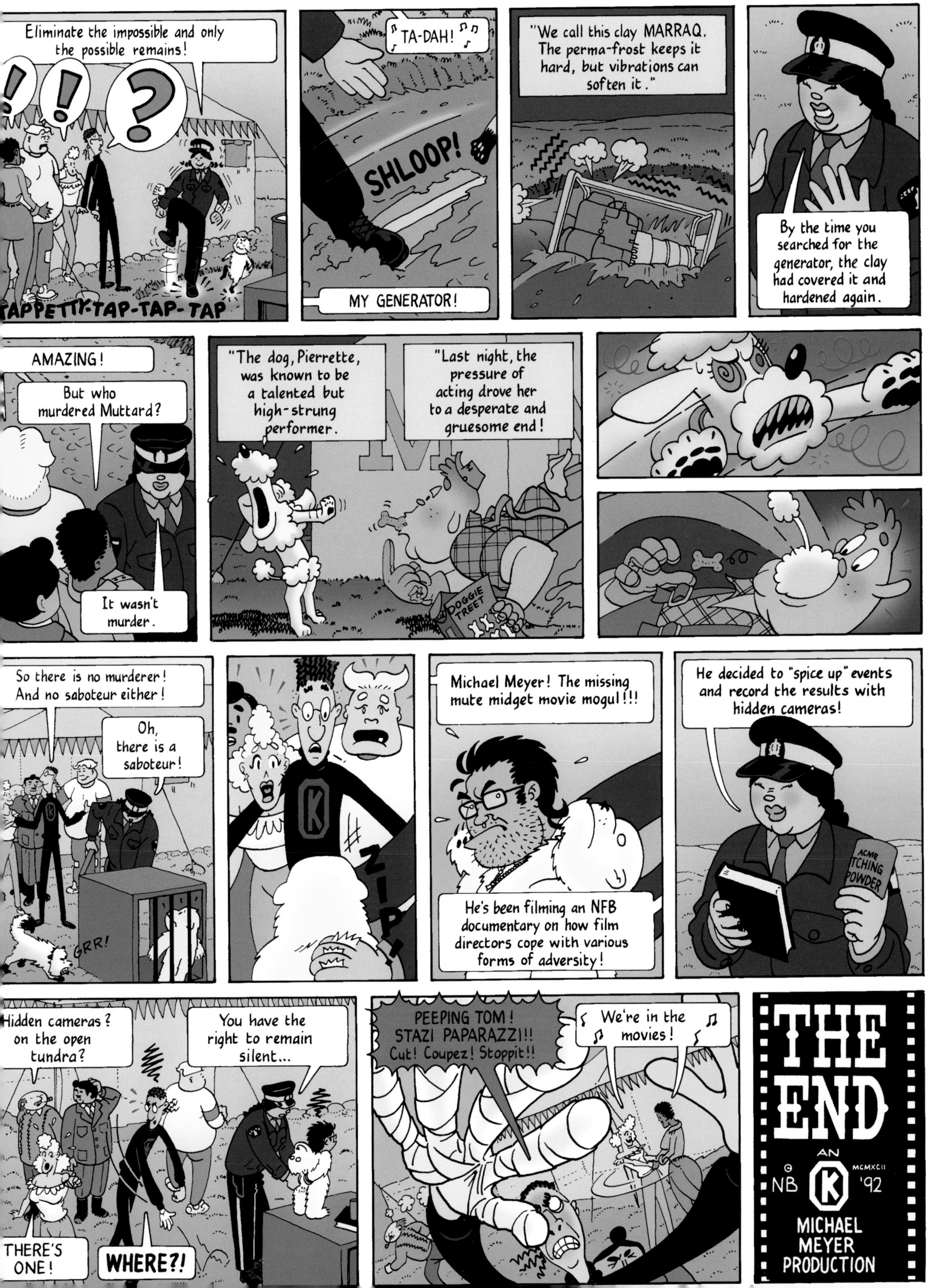
Eliminate the impossible and only the possible remains!
!
!
?
TAPPETTY-TAP-TAP-TAP
TA-DAH!
SHLOOP!
MY GENERATOR!
"We call this clay MARRAQ. The perma-frost keeps it hard, but vibrations can soften it."
By the time you searched for the generator, the clay had covered it and hardened again.
AMAZING!
But who murdered Muttard?
It wasn't murder.
"The dog, Pierrette, was known to be a talented but high-strung performer.
"Last night, the pressure of acting drove her to a desperate and gruesome end!
DOGGIE TREET
So there is no murderer! And no saboteur either!
Oh, there is a saboteur!
GRR!
ZIP!
Michael Meyer! The missing mute midget movie mogul!!!
He's been filming an NFB documentary on how film directors cope with various forms of adversity!
He decided to "spice up" events and record the results with hidden cameras!
ACME ITCHING POWDER
Hidden cameras? on the open tundra?
You have the right to remain silent...
THERE'S ONE!
WHERE?!
PEEPING TOM! STAZI PAPARAZZI!! Cut! Coupez! Stoppit!!
We're in the movies!
THE END
AN
© NB
MCMXCII '92
K
MICHAEL MEYER PRODUCTION

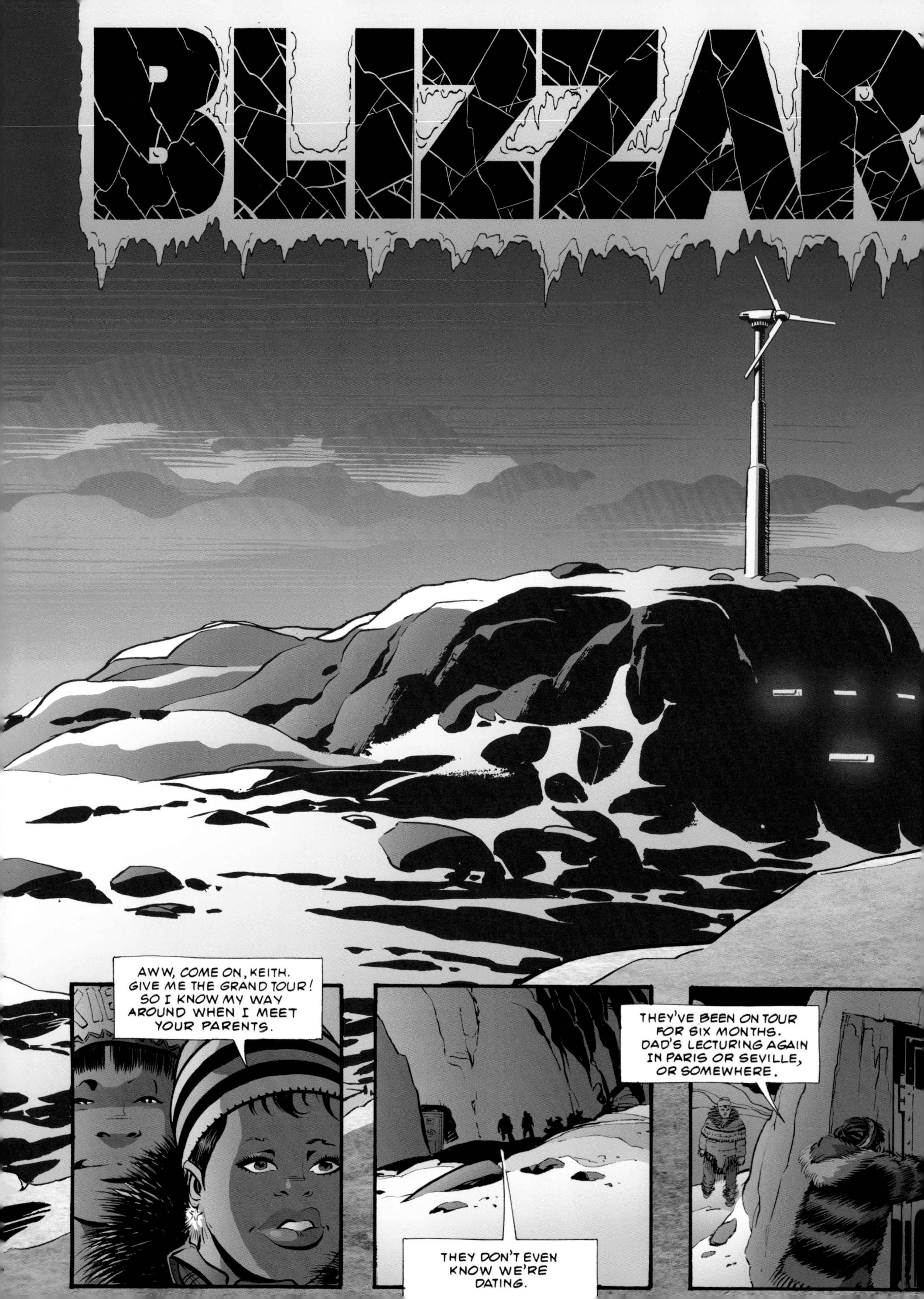
BLIZZAR
AWW, COME ON, KEITH. GIVE ME THE GRAND TOUR! SO I KNOW MY WAY AROUND WHEN I MEET YOUR PARENTS.
THEY DON'T EVEN KNOW WE'RE DATING.
THEY'VE BEEN ON TOUR FOR SIX MONTHS. DAD'S LECTURING AGAIN IN PARIS OR SEVILLE, OR SOMEWHERE.

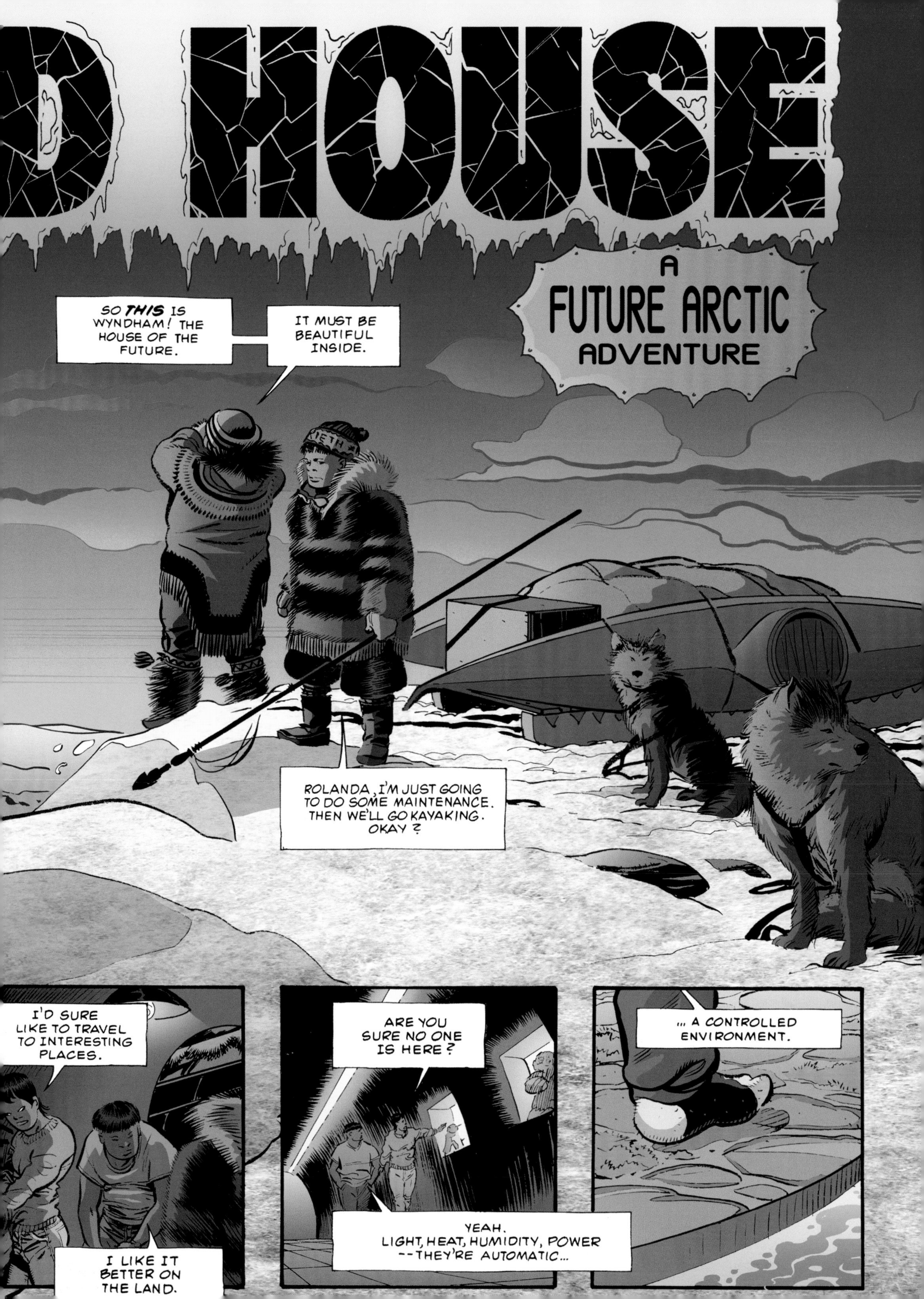
D HOUSE
A FUTURE ARCTIC ADVENTURE
SO THIS IS WYNDHAM! THE HOUSE OF THE FUTURE.
IT MUST BE BEAUTIFUL INSIDE.
ROLANDA, I'M JUST GOING TO DO SOME MAINTENANCE. THEN WE'LL GO KAYAKING. OKAY?
I'D SURE LIKE TO TRAVEL TO INTERESTING PLACES.
I LIKE IT BETTER ON THE LAND.
ARE YOU SURE NO ONE IS HERE?
YEAH. LIGHT, HEAT, HUMIDITY, POWER --THEY'RE AUTOMATIC...
... A CONTROLLED ENVIRONMENT.

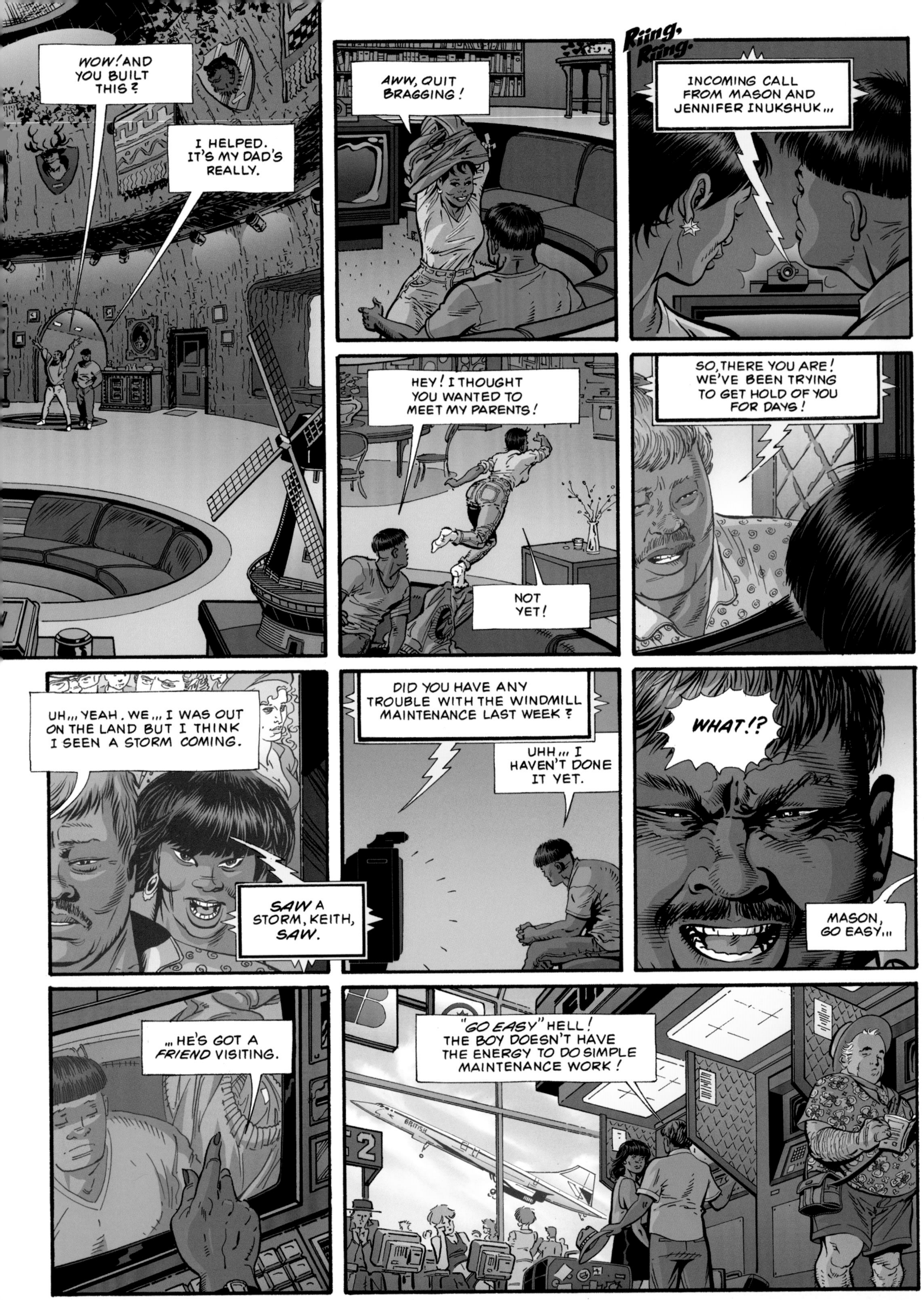
WOW! AND YOU BUILT THIS?
I HELPED. IT'S MY DAD'S REALLY.
AWW, QUIT BRAGGING!
Riing. Riing.
INCOMING CALL FROM MASON AND JENNIFER INUKSHUK...
HEY! I THOUGHT YOU WANTED TO MEET MY PARENTS!
NOT YET!
SO, THERE YOU ARE! WE'VE BEEN TRYING TO GET HOLD OF YOU FOR DAYS!
UH... YEAH. WE... I WAS OUT ON THE LAND BUT I THINK I SEEN A STORM COMING.
SAW A STORM, KEITH, SAW.
DID YOU HAVE ANY TROUBLE WITH THE WINDMILL MAINTENANCE LAST WEEK?
UHH... I HAVEN'T DONE IT YET.
WHAT!?
MASON, GO EASY...
...HE'S GOT A FRIEND VISITING.
"GO EASY" HELL! THE BOY DOESN'T HAVE THE ENERGY TO DO SIMPLE MAINTENANCE WORK!
BRITISH
2

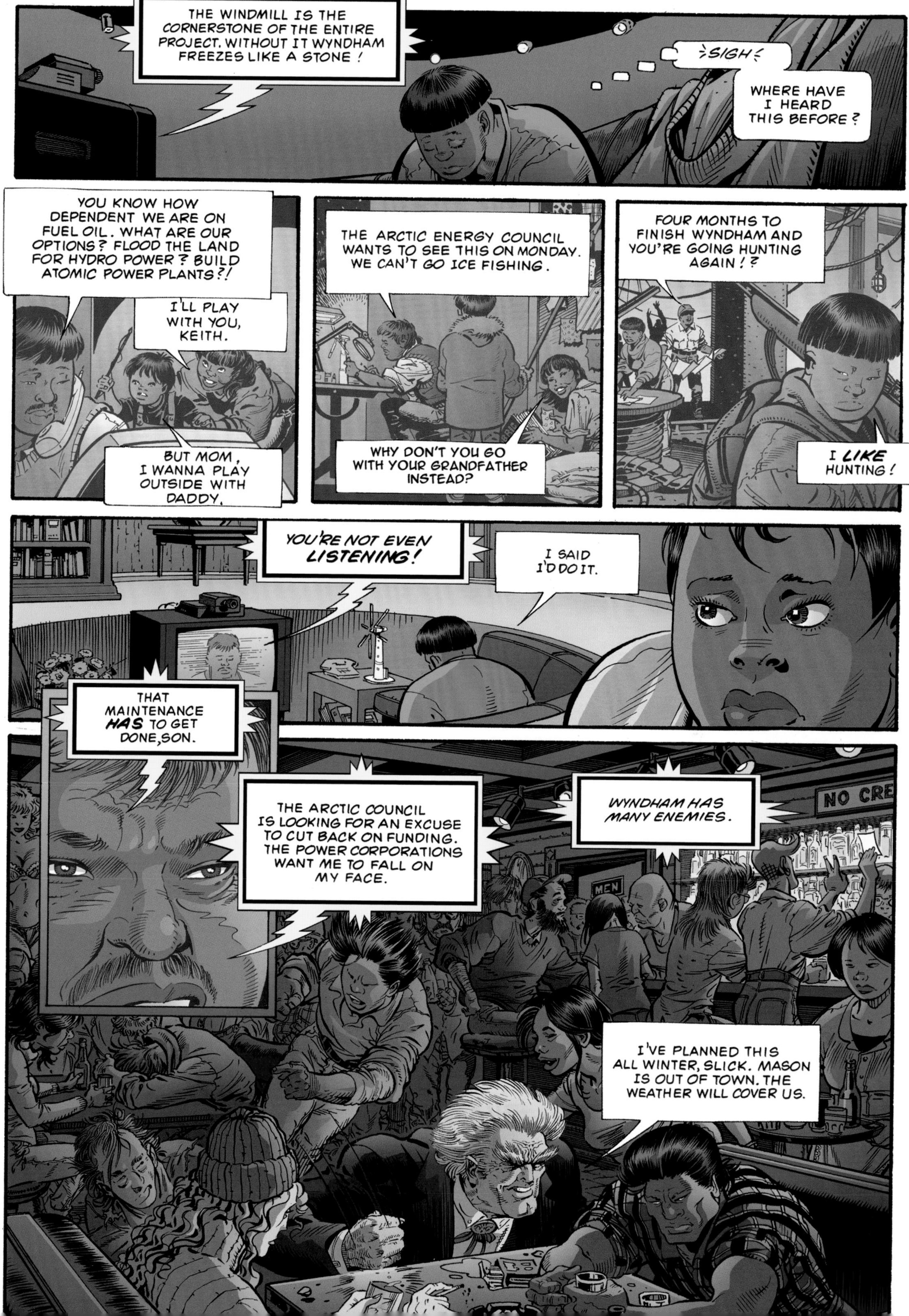
THE WINDMILL IS THE CORNERSTONE OF THE ENTIRE PROJECT. WITHOUT IT WYNDHAM FREEZES LIKE A STONE!
SIGH
WHERE HAVE I HEARD THIS BEFORE?
YOU KNOW HOW DEPENDENT WE ARE ON FUEL OIL. WHAT ARE OUR OPTIONS? FLOOD THE LAND FOR HYDRO POWER? BUILD ATOMIC POWER PLANTS?!
I'LL PLAY WITH YOU, KEITH.
BUT MOM, I WANNA PLAY OUTSIDE WITH DADDY.
THE ARCTIC ENERGY COUNCIL WANTS TO SEE THIS ON MONDAY. WE CAN'T GO ICE FISHING.
WHY DON'T YOU GO WITH YOUR GRANDFATHER INSTEAD?
FOUR MONTHS TO FINISH WYNDHAM AND YOU'RE GOING HUNTING AGAIN!?
I LIKE HUNTING!
YOU'RE NOT EVEN LISTENING!
I SAID I'D DO IT.
THAT MAINTENANCE HAS TO GET DONE, SON.
THE ARCTIC COUNCIL IS LOOKING FOR AN EXCUSE TO CUT BACK ON FUNDING. THE POWER CORPORATIONS WANT ME TO FALL ON MY FACE.
WYNDHAM HAS MANY ENEMIES.
NO CRE
MEN
I'VE PLANNED THIS ALL WINTER, SLICK. MASON IS OUT OF TOWN. THE WEATHER WILL COVER US.

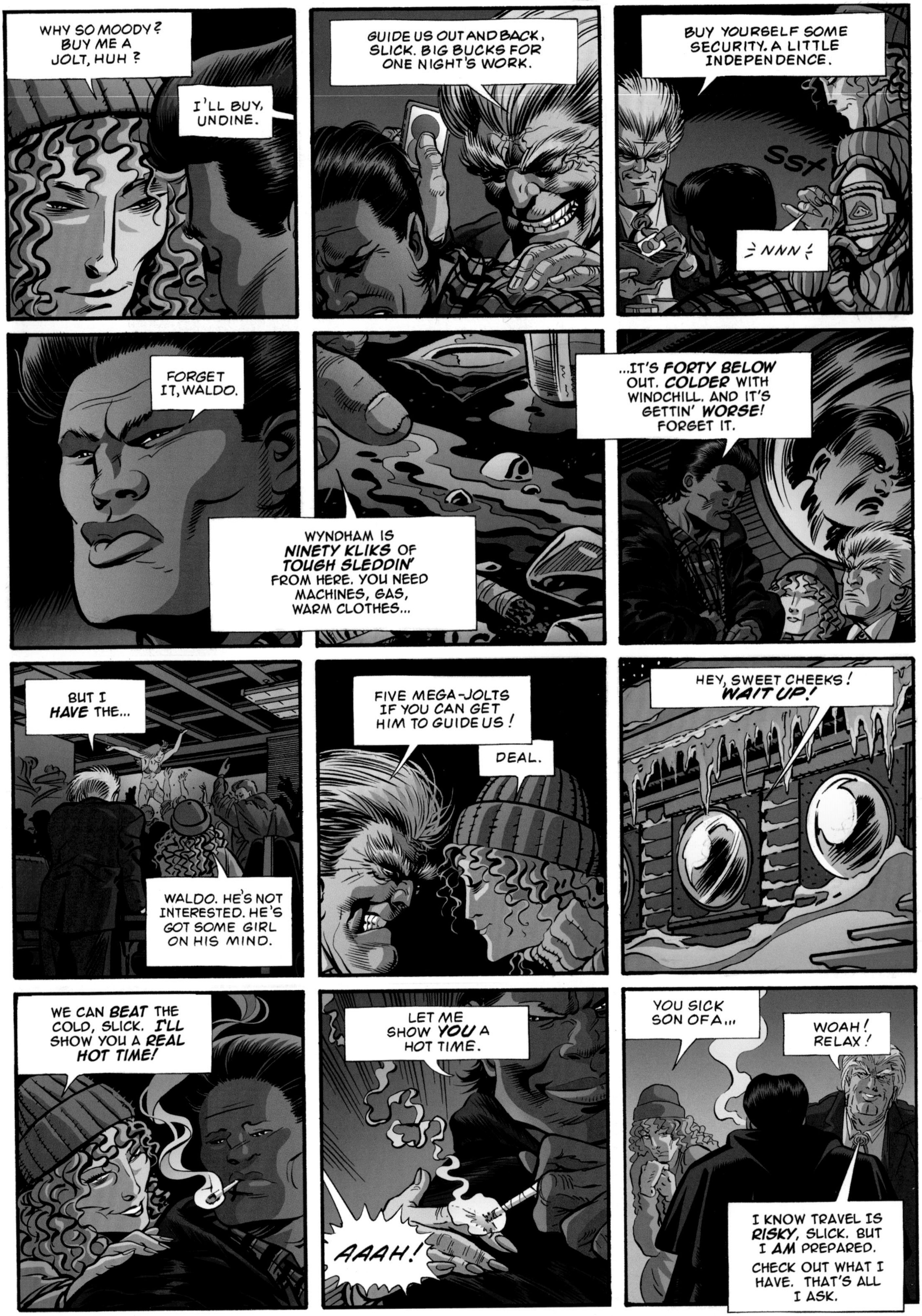

WHY SO MOODY? BUY ME A JOLT, HUH?
I'LL BUY, UNDINE.
GUIDE US OUT AND BACK, SLICK. BIG BUCKS FOR ONE NIGHT'S WORK.
BUY YOURSELF SOME SECURITY. A LITTLE INDEPENDENCE.
SSST
NNN
FORGET IT, WALDO.
WYNDHAM IS NINETY KLIKS OF TOUGH SLEDDIN' FROM HERE. YOU NEED MACHINES, GAS, WARM CLOTHES...
...IT'S FORTY BELOW OUT. COLDER WITH WINDCHILL. AND IT'S GETTIN' WORSE! FORGET IT.
BUT I HAVE THE...
WALDO. HE'S NOT INTERESTED. HE'S GOT SOME GIRL ON HIS MIND.
FIVE MEGA-JOLTS IF YOU CAN GET HIM TO GUIDE US!
DEAL.
HEY, SWEET CHEEKS! WAIT UP!
WE CAN BEAT THE COLD, SLICK. I'LL SHOW YOU A REAL HOT TIME!
LET ME SHOW YOU A HOT TIME.
AAAH!
YOU SICK SON OF A...
WOAH! RELAX!
I KNOW TRAVEL IS RISKY, SLICK. BUT I AM PREPARED.
CHECK OUT WHAT I HAVE. THAT'S ALL I ASK.

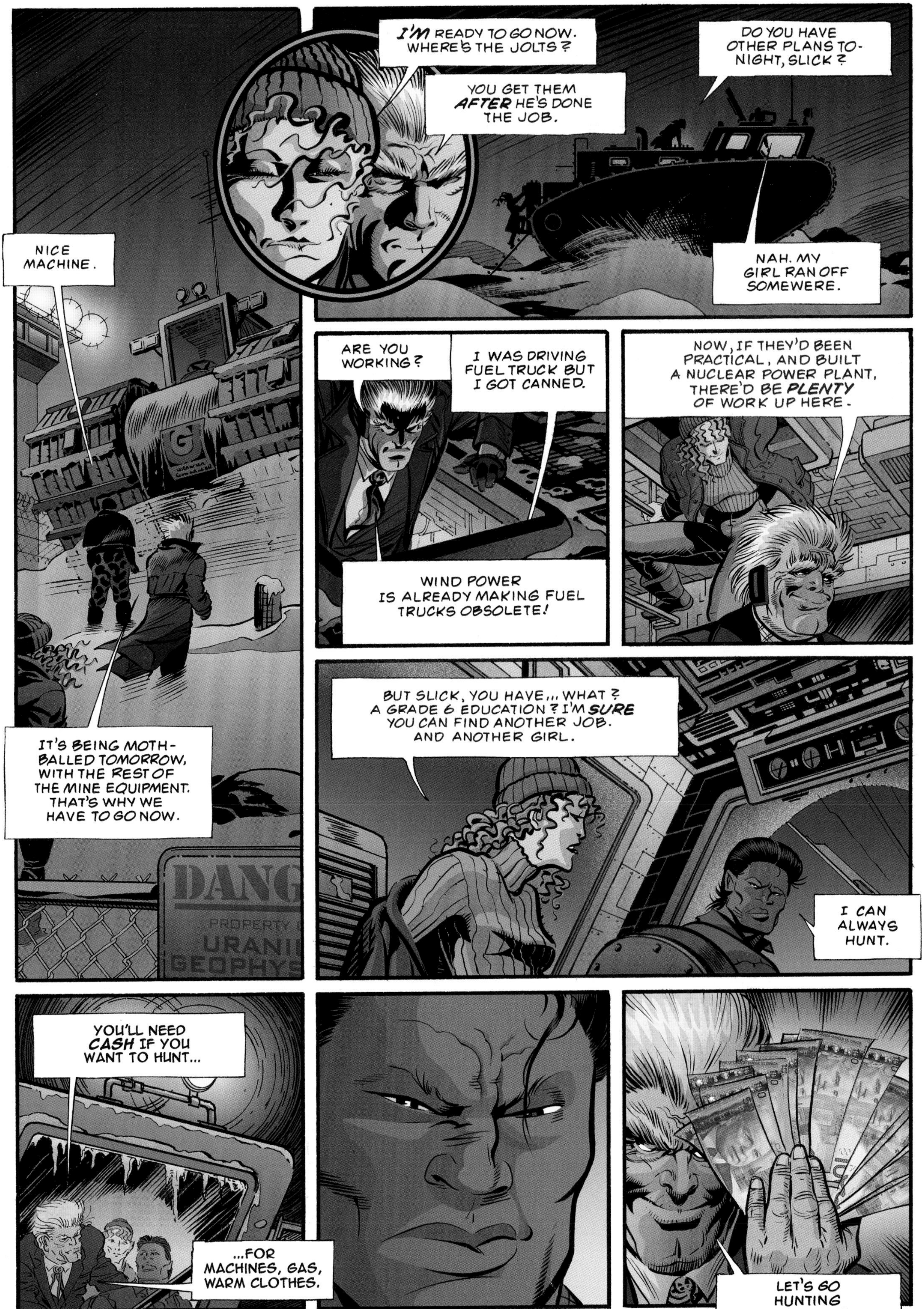

I'M READY TO GO NOW. WHERE'S THE JOLTS?
YOU GET THEM AFTER HE'S DONE THE JOB.
DO YOU HAVE OTHER PLANS TO-NIGHT, SLICK?
NAH. MY GIRL RAN OFF SOMEWERE.
NICE MACHINE.
IT'S BEING MOTH-BALLED TOMORROW, WITH THE REST OF THE MINE EQUIPMENT. THAT'S WHY WE HAVE TO GO NOW.
DANG
PROPERTY O
URANI
GEOPHYS
ARE YOU WORKING?
I WAS DRIVING FUEL TRUCK BUT I GOT CANNED.
WIND POWER IS ALREADY MAKING FUEL TRUCKS OBSOLETE!
NOW, IF THEY'D BEEN PRACTICAL, AND BUILT A NUCLEAR POWER PLANT, THERE'D BE PLENTY OF WORK UP HERE.
BUT SLICK, YOU HAVE... WHAT? A GRADE 6 EDUCATION? I'M SURE YOU CAN FIND ANOTHER JOB. AND ANOTHER GIRL.
I CAN ALWAYS HUNT.
YOU'LL NEED CASH IF YOU WANT TO HUNT...
...FOR MACHINES, GAS, WARM CLOTHES.
LET'S GO HUNTING WINDMILLS.

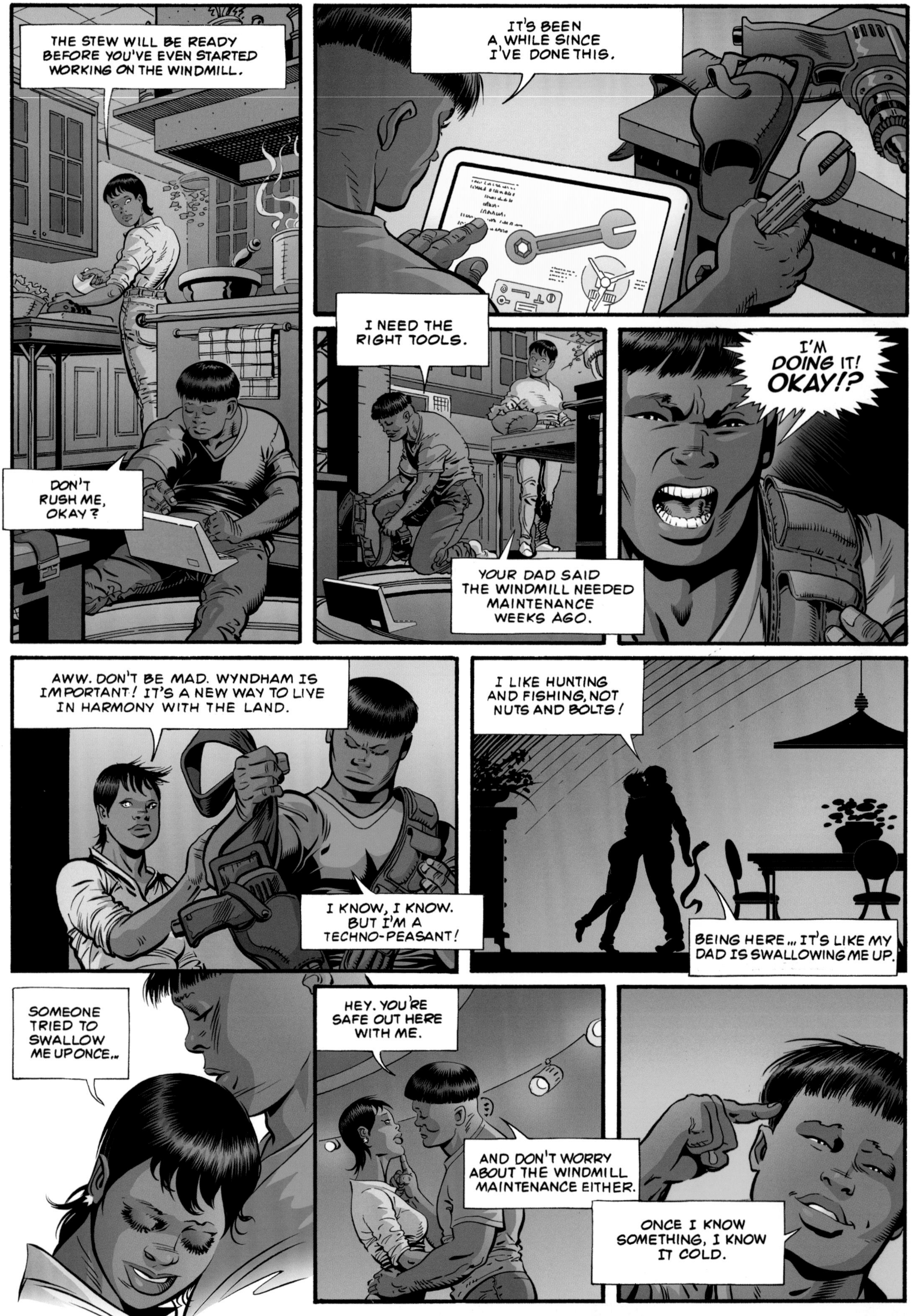
THE STEW WILL BE READY BEFORE YOU'VE EVEN STARTED WORKING ON THE WINDMILL.
DON'T RUSH ME, OKAY?
IT'S BEEN A WHILE SINCE I'VE DONE THIS.
I NEED THE RIGHT TOOLS.
YOUR DAD SAID THE WINDMILL NEEDED MAINTENANCE WEEKS AGO.
I'M DOING IT! OKAY!?
AWW. DON'T BE MAD. WYNDHAM IS IMPORTANT! IT'S A NEW WAY TO LIVE IN HARMONY WITH THE LAND.
I KNOW, I KNOW. BUT I'M A TECHNO-PEASANT!
I LIKE HUNTING AND FISHING, NOT NUTS AND BOLTS!
BEING HERE... IT'S LIKE MY DAD IS SWALLOWING ME UP.
SOMEONE TRIED TO SWALLOW ME UP ONCE...
HEY. YOU'RE SAFE OUT HERE WITH ME.
AND DON'T WORRY ABOUT THE WINDMILL MAINTENANCE EITHER.
ONCE I KNOW SOMETHING, I KNOW IT COLD.

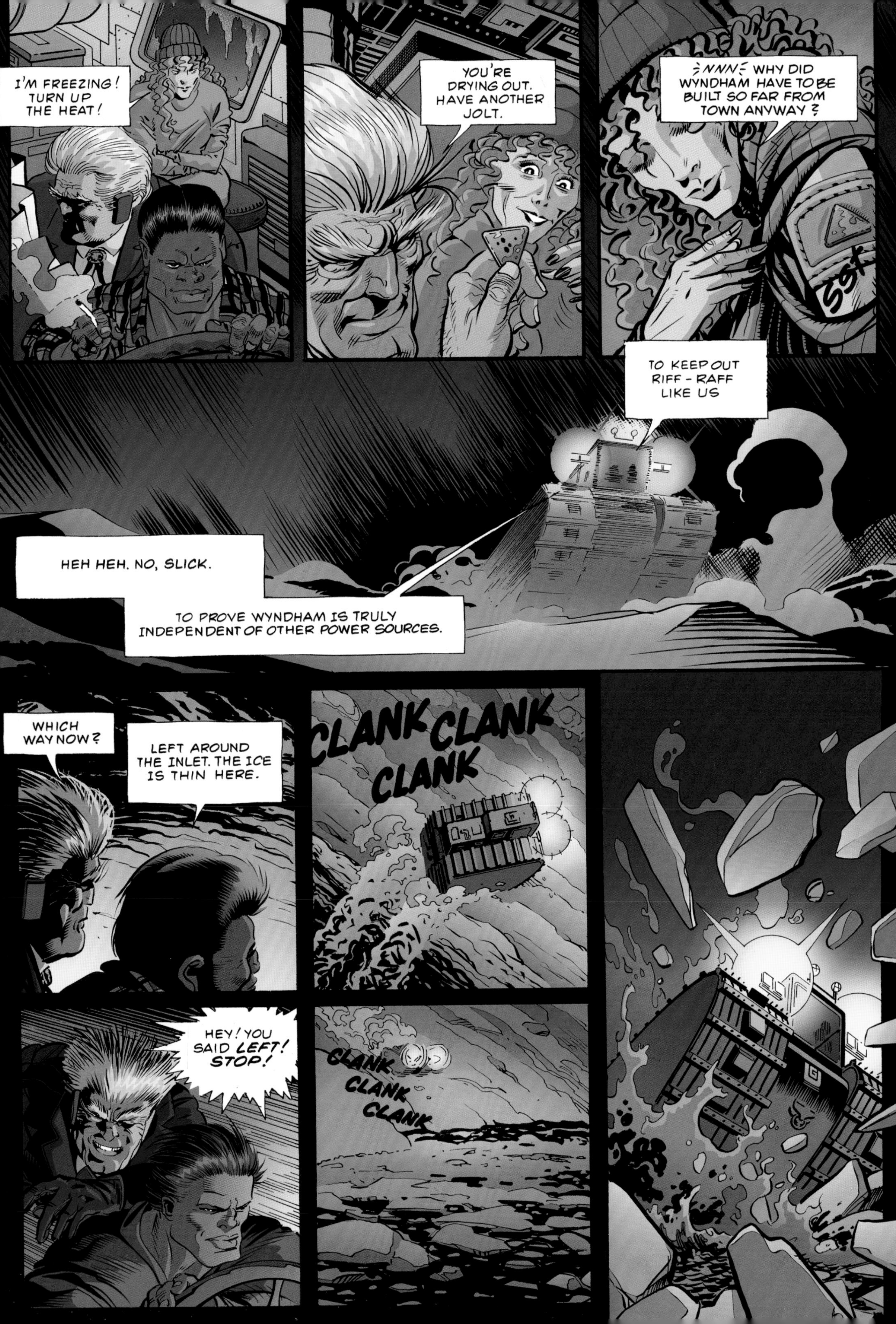
I'M FREEZING! TURN UP THE HEAT!
YOU'RE DRYING OUT. HAVE ANOTHER JOLT.
NNN! WHY DID WYNDHAM HAVE TO BE BUILT SO FAR FROM TOWN ANYWAY?
TO KEEP OUT RIFF - RAFF LIKE US
HEH HEH. NO, SLICK.
TO PROVE WYNDHAM IS TRULY INDEPENDENT OF OTHER POWER SOURCES.
WHICH WAY NOW?
LEFT AROUND THE INLET. THE ICE IS THIN HERE.
CLANK CLANK CLANK
HEY! YOU SAID LEFT! STOP!
CLANK CLANK CLANK

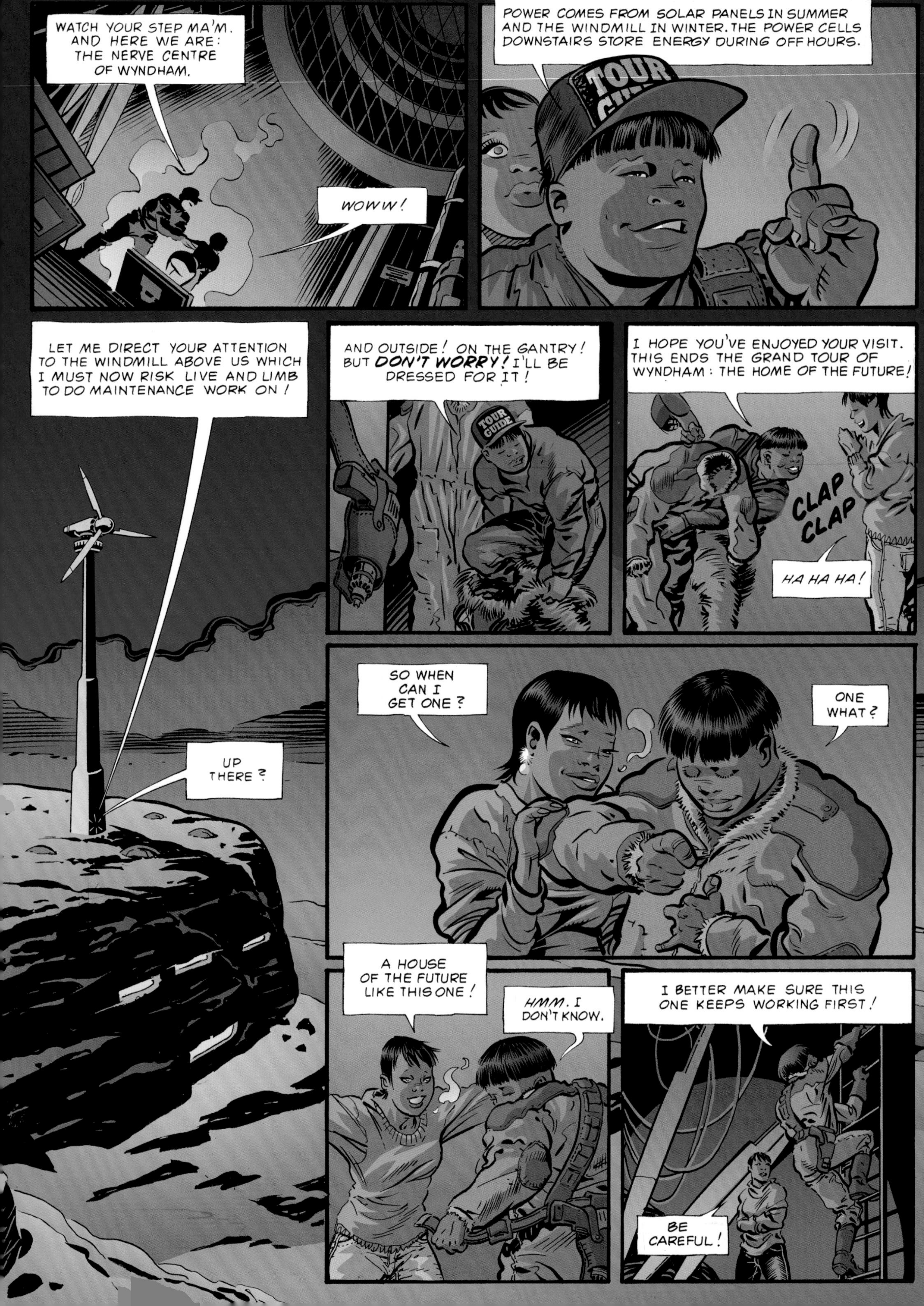
WATCH YOUR STEP MA'M. AND HERE WE ARE: THE NERVE CENTRE OF WYNDHAM.
WOWW!
POWER COMES FROM SOLAR PANELS IN SUMMER AND THE WINDMILL IN WINTER. THE POWER CELLS DOWNSTAIRS STORE ENERGY DURING OFF HOURS.
TOUR GUIDE
LET ME DIRECT YOUR ATTENTION TO THE WINDMILL ABOVE US WHICH I MUST NOW RISK LIVE AND LIMB TO DO MAINTENANCE WORK ON!
UP THERE?
AND OUTSIDE! ON THE GANTRY! BUT DON'T WORRY! I'LL BE DRESSED FOR IT!
TOUR GUIDE
I HOPE YOU'VE ENJOYED YOUR VISIT. THIS ENDS THE GRAND TOUR OF WYNDHAM: THE HOME OF THE FUTURE!
CLAP CLAP
HA HA HA!
SO WHEN CAN I GET ONE?
ONE WHAT?
A HOUSE OF THE FUTURE LIKE THIS ONE!
HMM. I DON'T KNOW.
I BETTER MAKE SURE THIS ONE KEEPS WORKING FIRST!
BE CAREFUL!

I THOUGHT WE WERE DEAD!

RELAX. THIS BABY IS AMPHIBIOUS.

WHY GO AROUND THE INLET WHEN WE CAN GO THROUGH IT?

HMM. YES. WHY WASTE *ENERGY*?

WYNDHAM — HOME OF THE FUTURE

YOU HAVE URANIUM IN YOUR OWN BACKYARD! ATOMIC POWER IS ARCTIC POWER!

ATOMIC POWER

HYDRO

THANK YOU MR. HALBERT. THE *ARCTIC COUNCIL* IS CONSIDERING ALL THE OPTIONS.

*@#¢¢ PASSIVE ENERGY! EVERYTHING I OWN IS TIED UP IN ATOMIC POWER!

TECHNOLOGY ISN'T PRE-ORDAINED, WALDO.

SURE THERE'S ALWAYS GOING TO BE PROGRESS... BUT IT DOESN'T HAVE TO BE *OUR* IDEA OF PROGRESS.

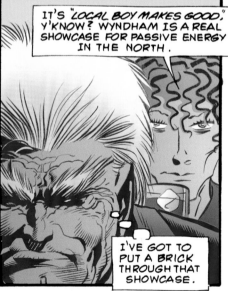

IT'S "LOCAL BOY MAKES GOOD," Y'KNOW? WYNDHAM IS A REAL SHOWCASE FOR PASSIVE ENERGY IN THE NORTH.

I'VE GOT TO PUT A BRICK THROUGH THAT SHOWCASE.

WE'RE THERE.

GOOD, SLICK. YOU AND UNDINE WAIT HERE. I'LL TAKE CARE OF THIS PERSONALLY.

SO FAR SO GOOD.

IT'LL LOOK LIKE THE TOWER COLLAPSED IN THE WIND...

... IF I SET OFF THE BOMB HERE!

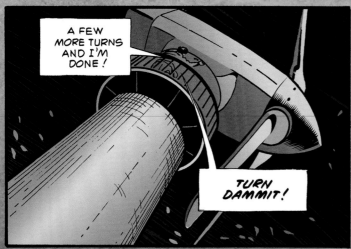

A FEW MORE TURNS AND I'M DONE!

TURN DAMMIT!

BLENG!

OOPS!

GOTCHA!

?

01:00

HELLO?

UH... HELLO!

MY NAME'S RAY. I'M HERE TO INSPECT THE WINDMILL.

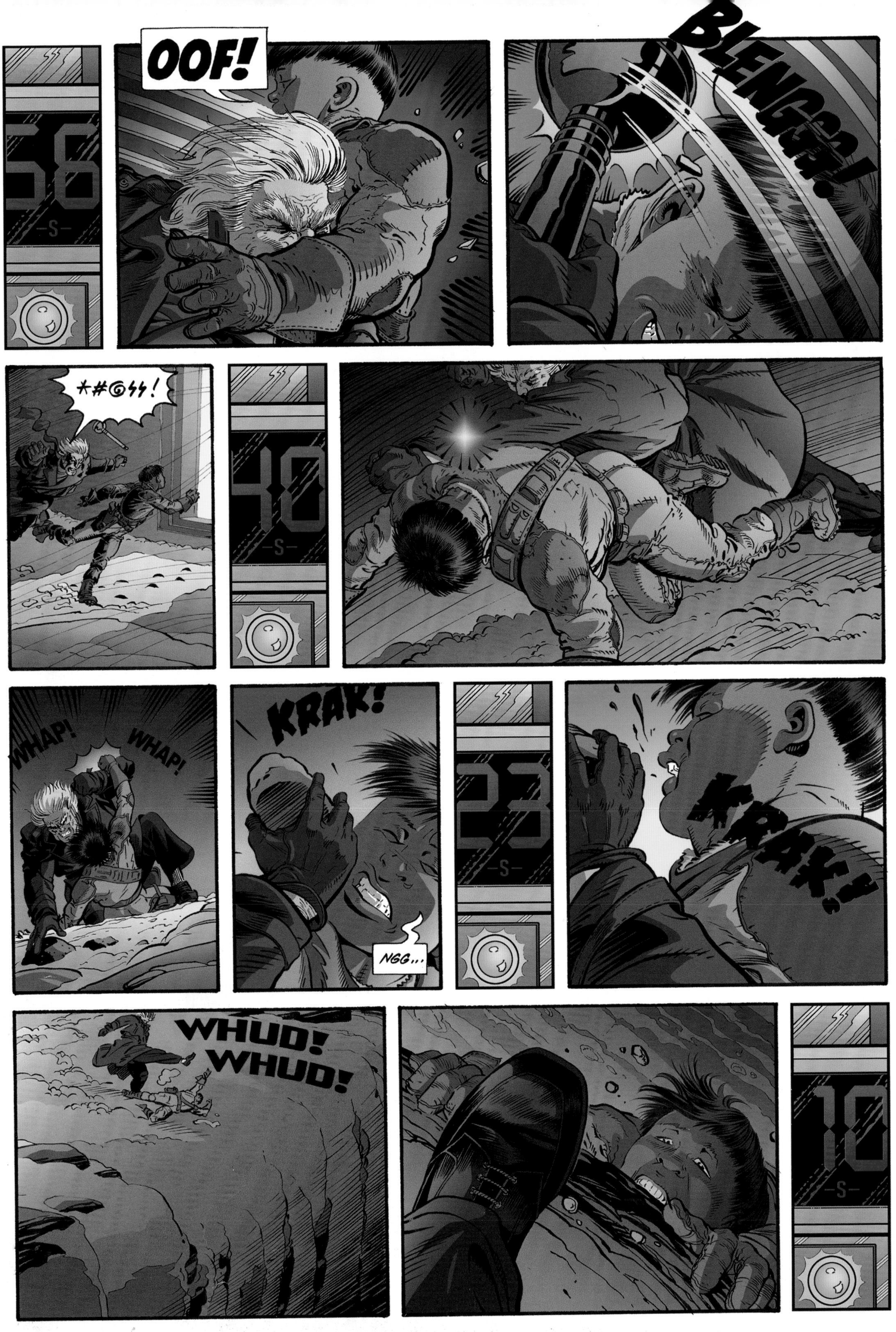
56
S
OOF!
BLENGGH!
*#@ϟϟ!
40
S
WHAP!
WHAP!
KRAK!
NGG...
23
S
KRAK!
WHUD!
WHUD!
10
S

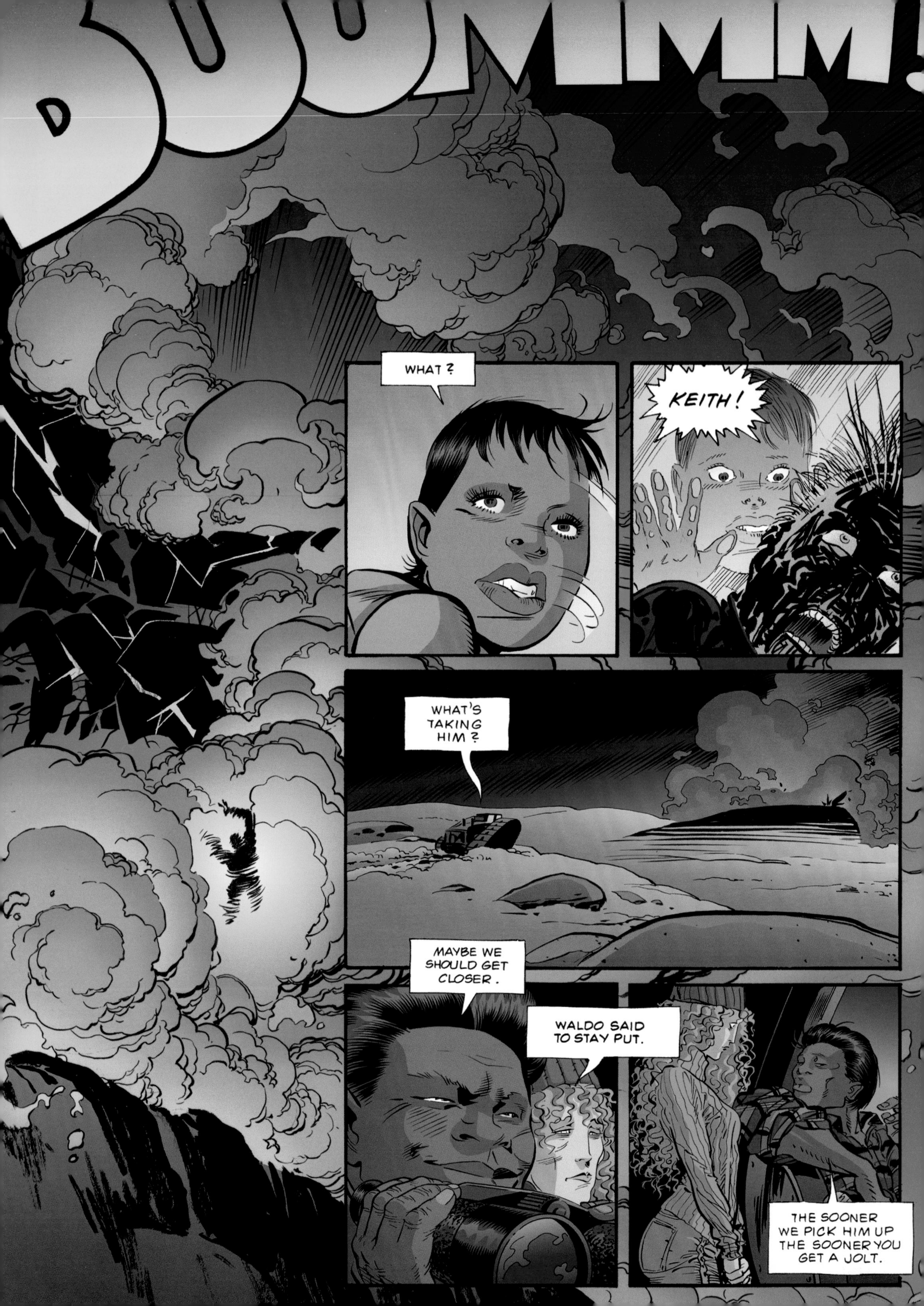
BUUMMM!
WHAT ?
KEITH !
WHAT'S TAKING HIM ?
MAYBE WE SHOULD GET CLOSER .
WALDO SAID TO STAY PUT.
THE SOONER WE PICK HIM UP THE SOONER YOU GET A JOLT.

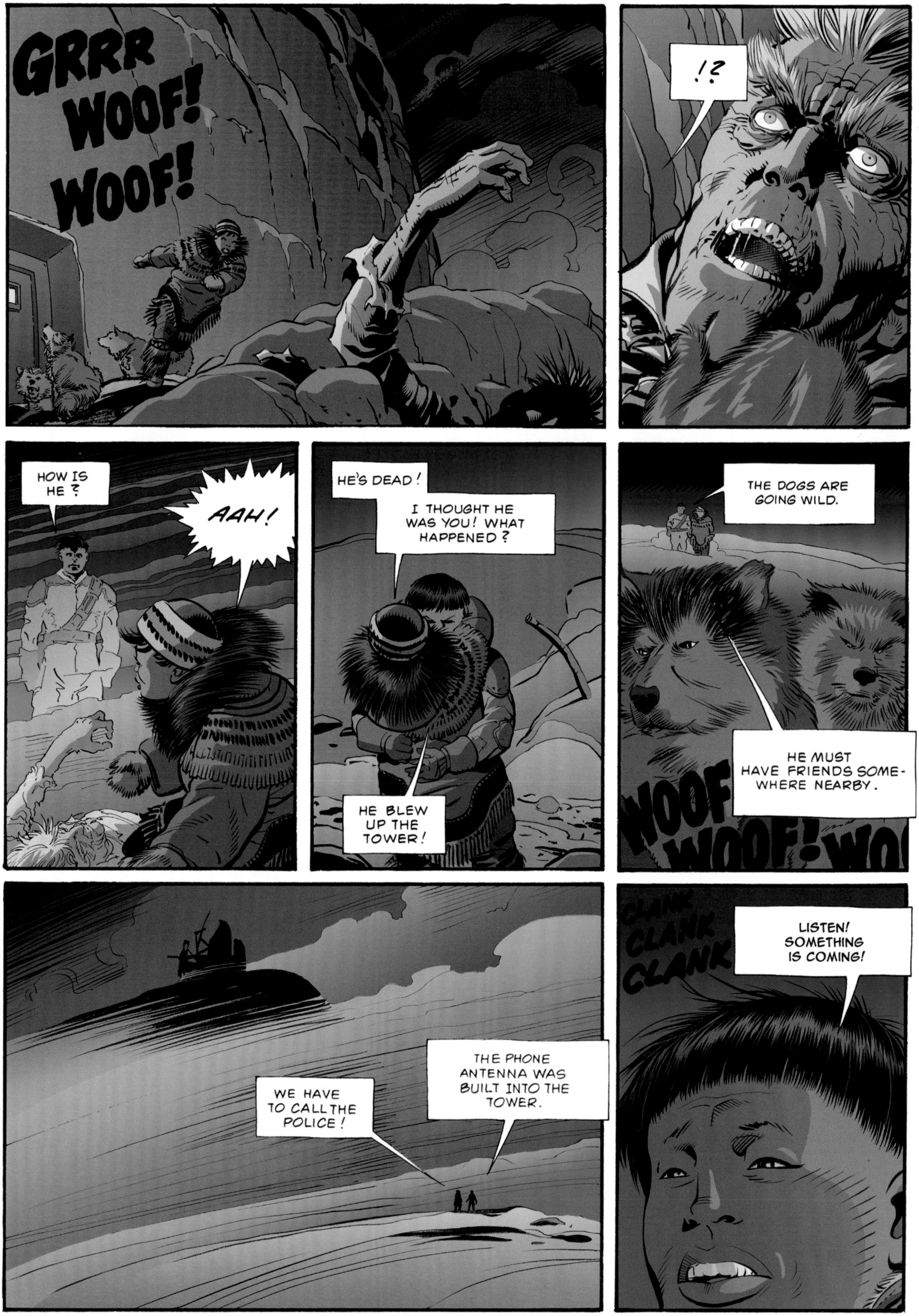
GRRR
WOOF!
WOOF!
!?
HOW IS HE ?
AAH!
HE'S DEAD!
I THOUGHT HE WAS YOU! WHAT HAPPENED ?
HE BLEW UP THE TOWER!
THE DOGS ARE GOING WILD.
HE MUST HAVE FRIENDS SOME-WHERE NEARBY.
WOOF
WOOF!
WE HAVE TO CALL THE POLICE !
THE PHONE ANTENNA WAS BUILT INTO THE TOWER.
CLANK
CLANK
CLANK
LISTEN! SOMETHING IS COMING!

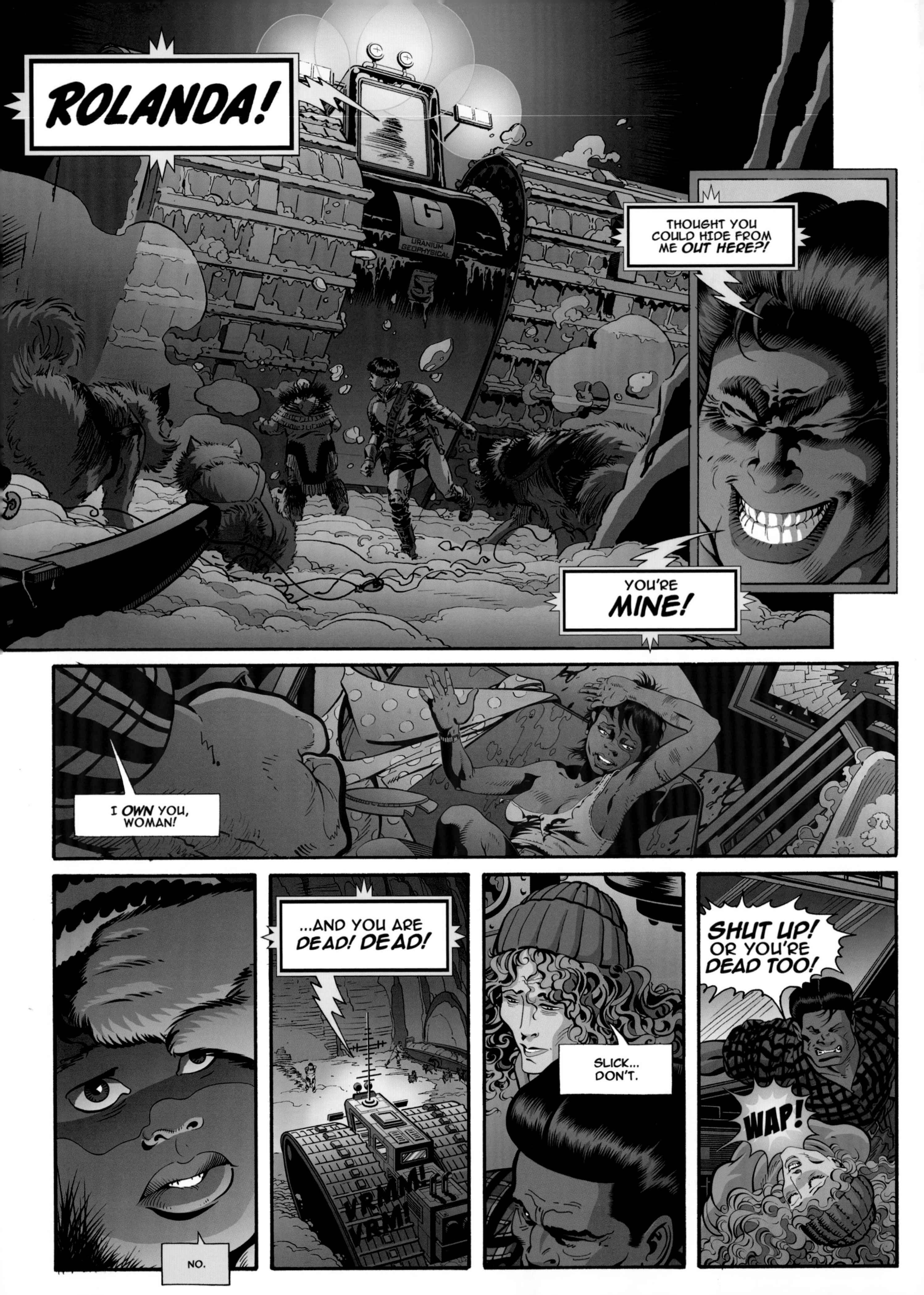
ROLANDA!
THOUGHT YOU COULD HIDE FROM ME OUT HERE?!
YOU'RE MINE!
I OWN YOU, WOMAN!
NO.
...AND YOU ARE DEAD! DEAD!
VRMM! VRM!
SLICK... DON'T.
SHUT UP! OR YOU'RE DEAD TOO!
WAP!

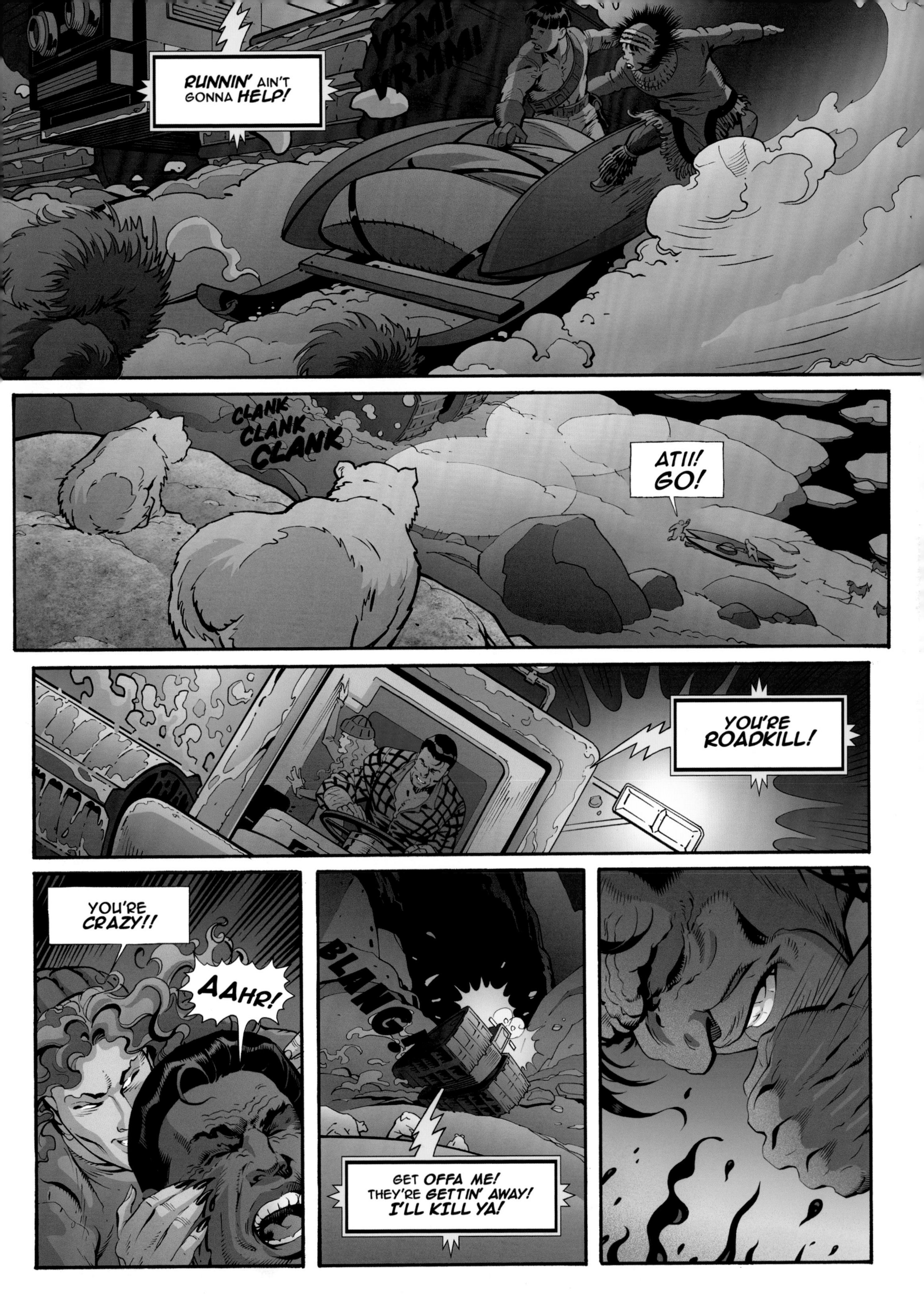
RUNNIN' AIN'T GONNA HELP!
VRM! VRMM!
CLANK CLANK CLANK
ATII! GO!
YOU'RE ROADKILL!
YOU'RE CRAZY!!
AAHR!
BLANG!
GET OFFA ME! THEY'RE GETTIN' AWAY! I'LL KILL YA!

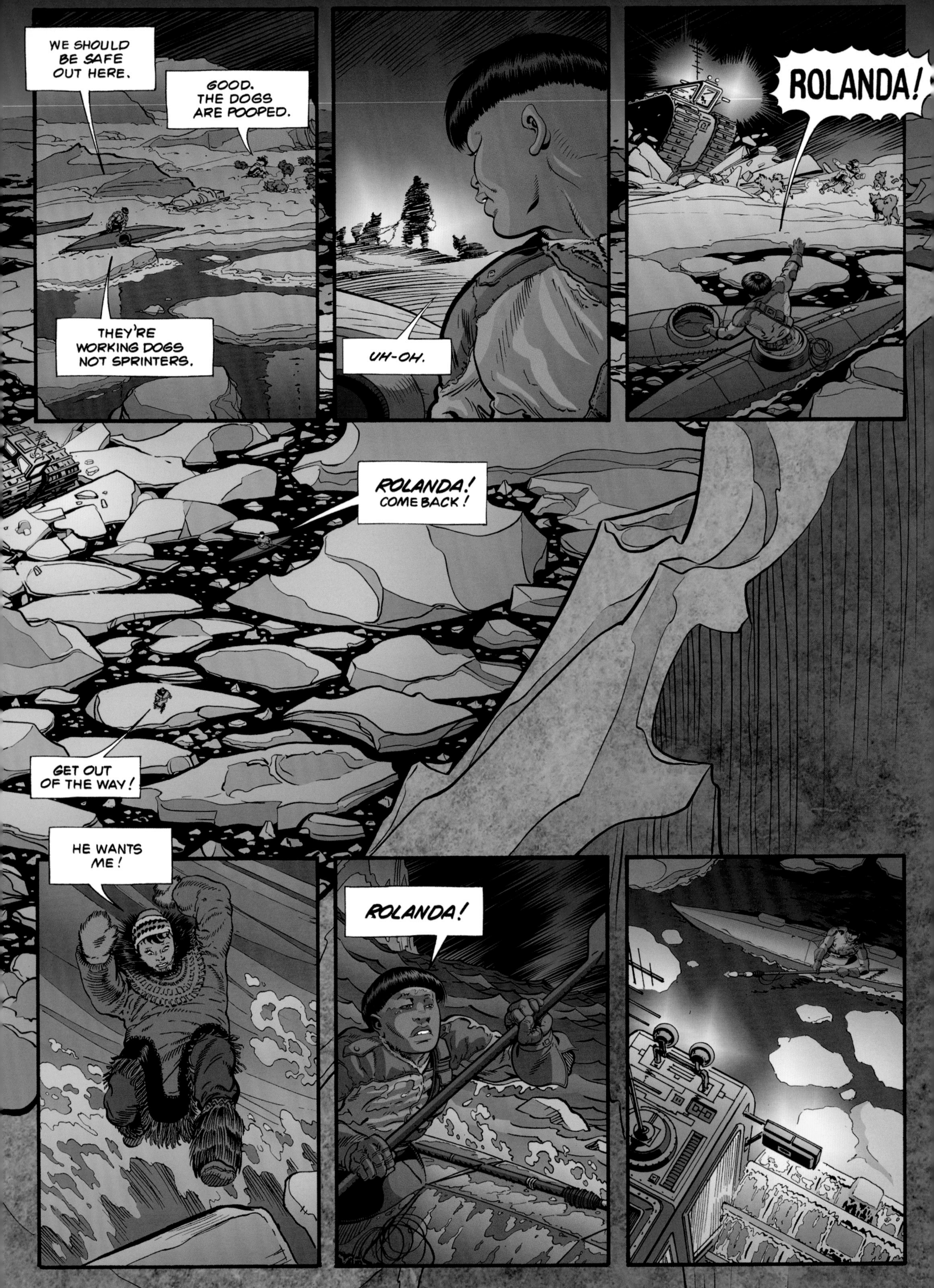
WE SHOULD BE SAFE OUT HERE.
GOOD. THE DOGS ARE POOPED.
THEY'RE WORKING DOGS NOT SPRINTERS.
UH-OH.
ROLANDA!
ROLANDA! COME BACK!
GET OUT OF THE WAY!
HE WANTS ME!
ROLANDA!

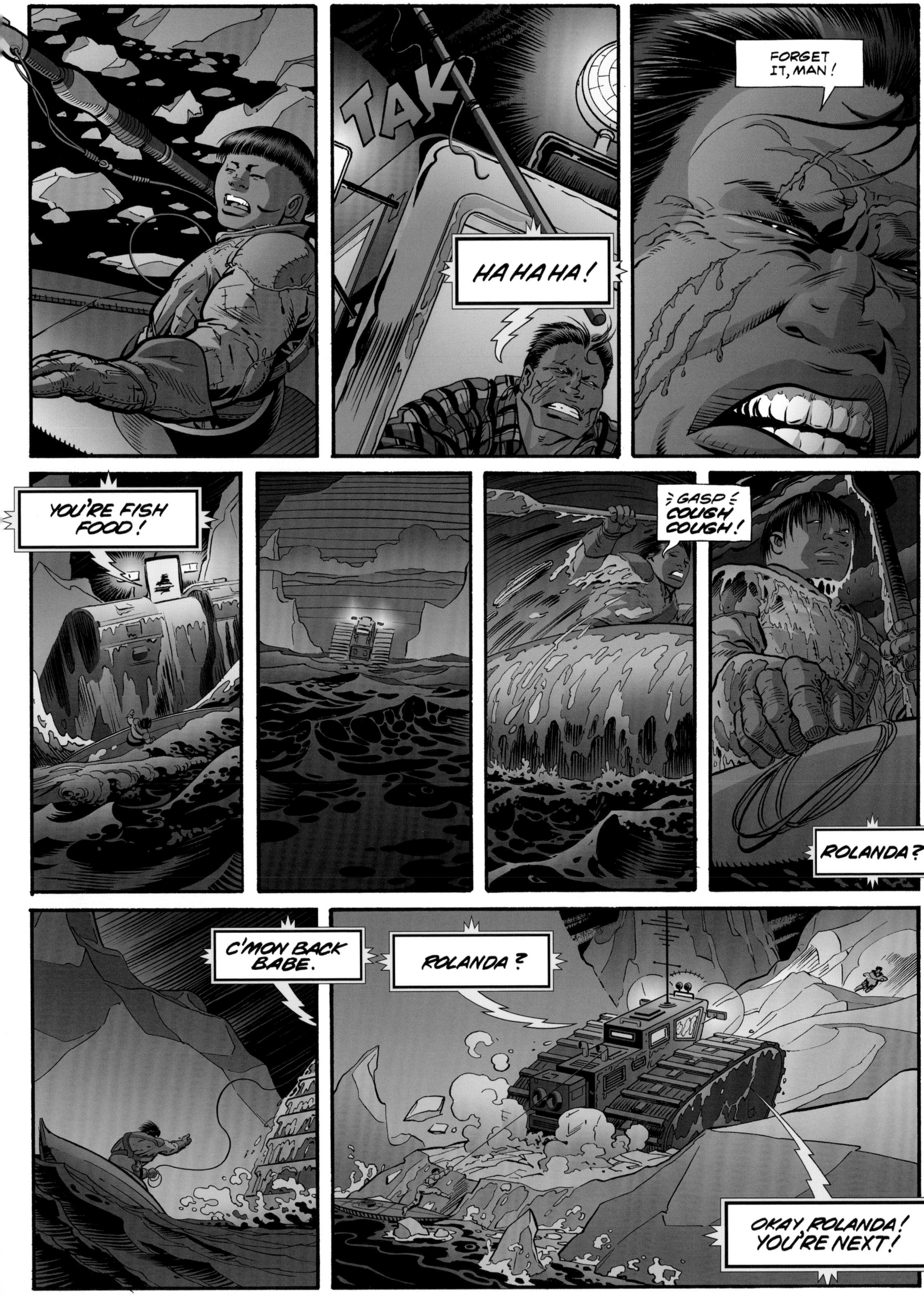
TAK
HA HA HA!
FORGET IT, MAN!
YOU'RE FISH FOOD!
GASP COUGH COUGH!
ROLANDA?
C'MON BACK BABE.
ROLANDA?
OKAY, ROLANDA! YOU'RE NEXT!

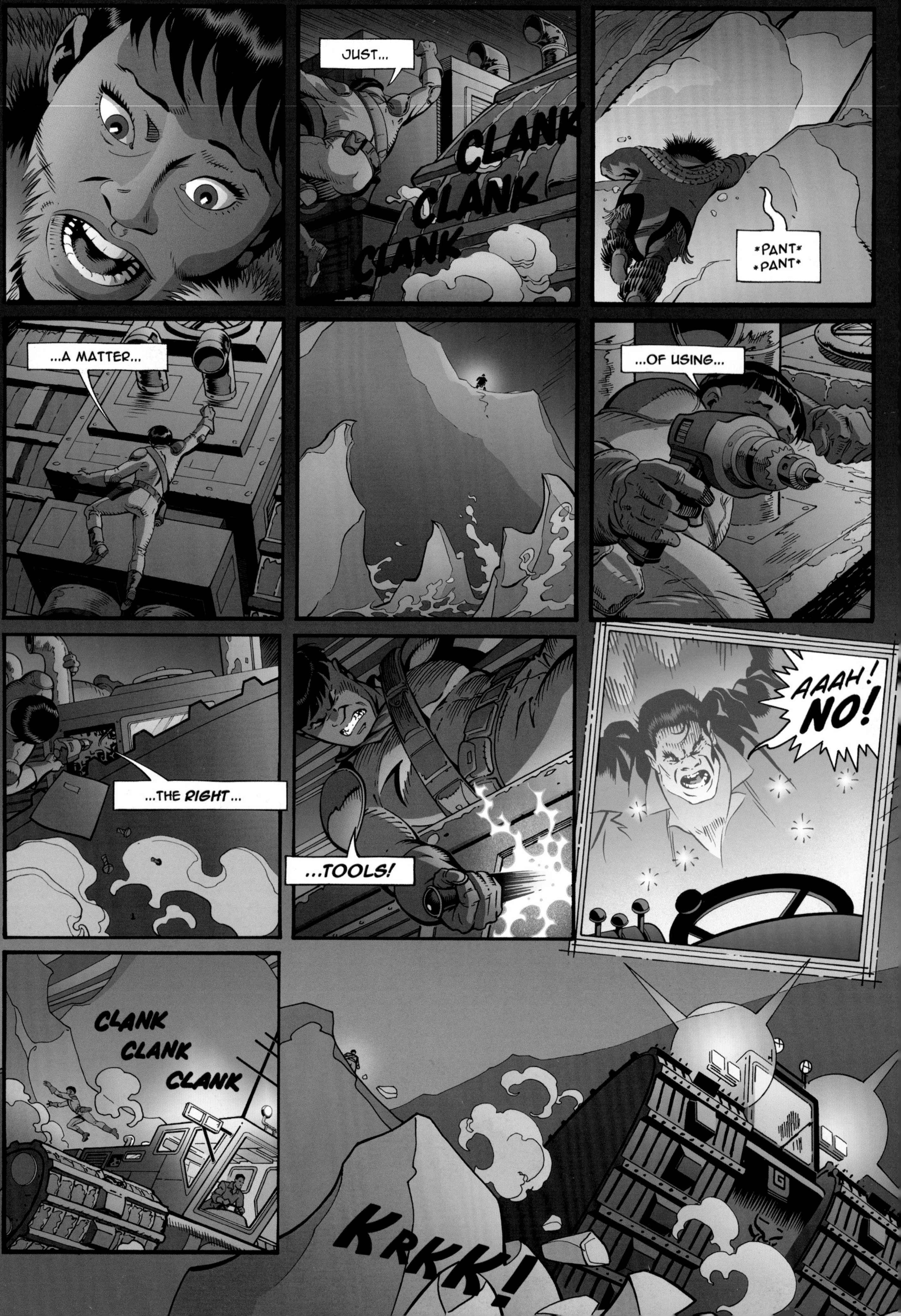
JUST...
CLANK
CLANK
CLANK
PANT
PANT
...A MATTER...
...OF USING...
...THE RIGHT...
...TOOLS!
AAAH!
NO!
CLANK
CLANK
CLANK
KRKK!

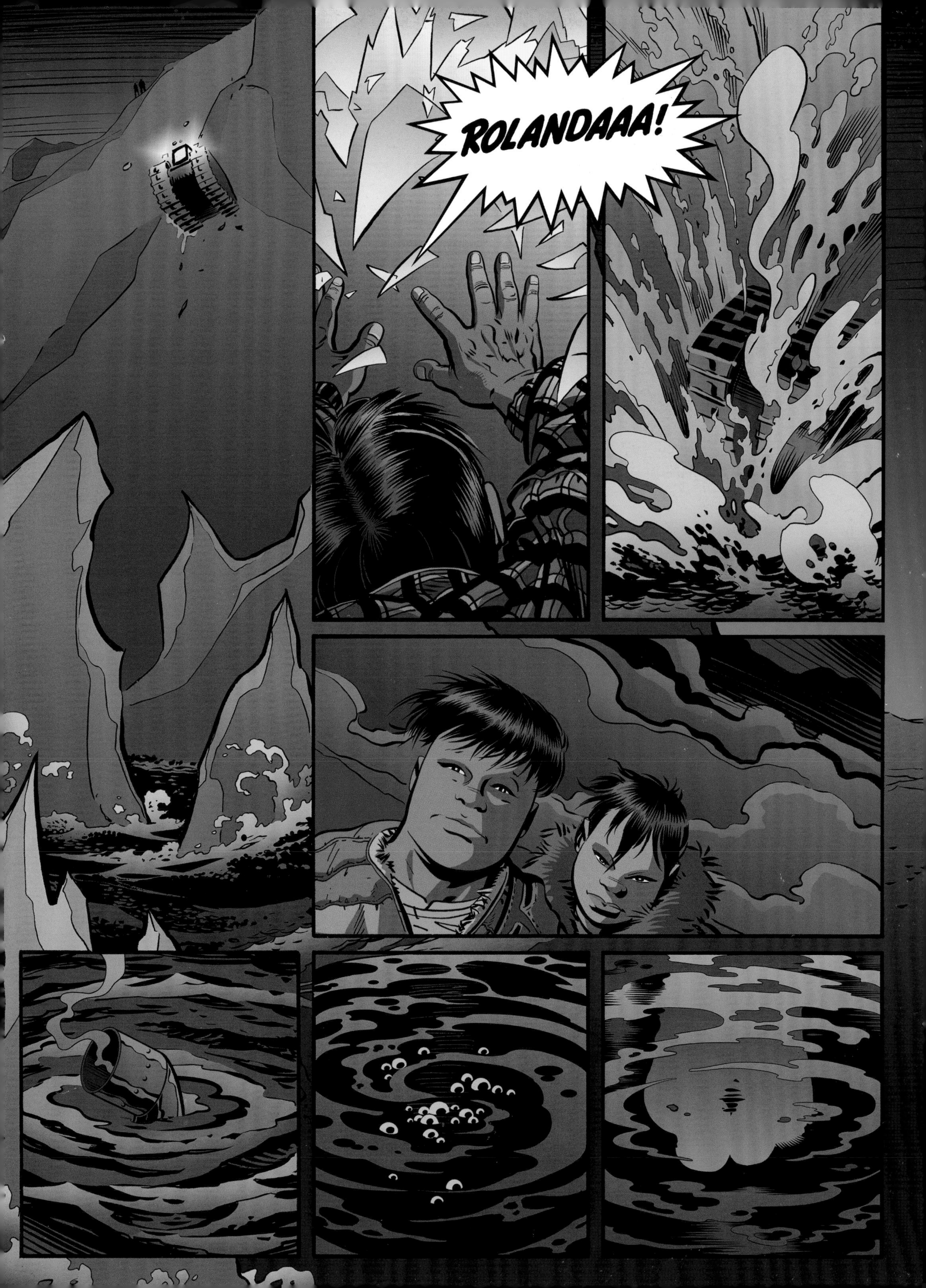
ROLANDAAA!

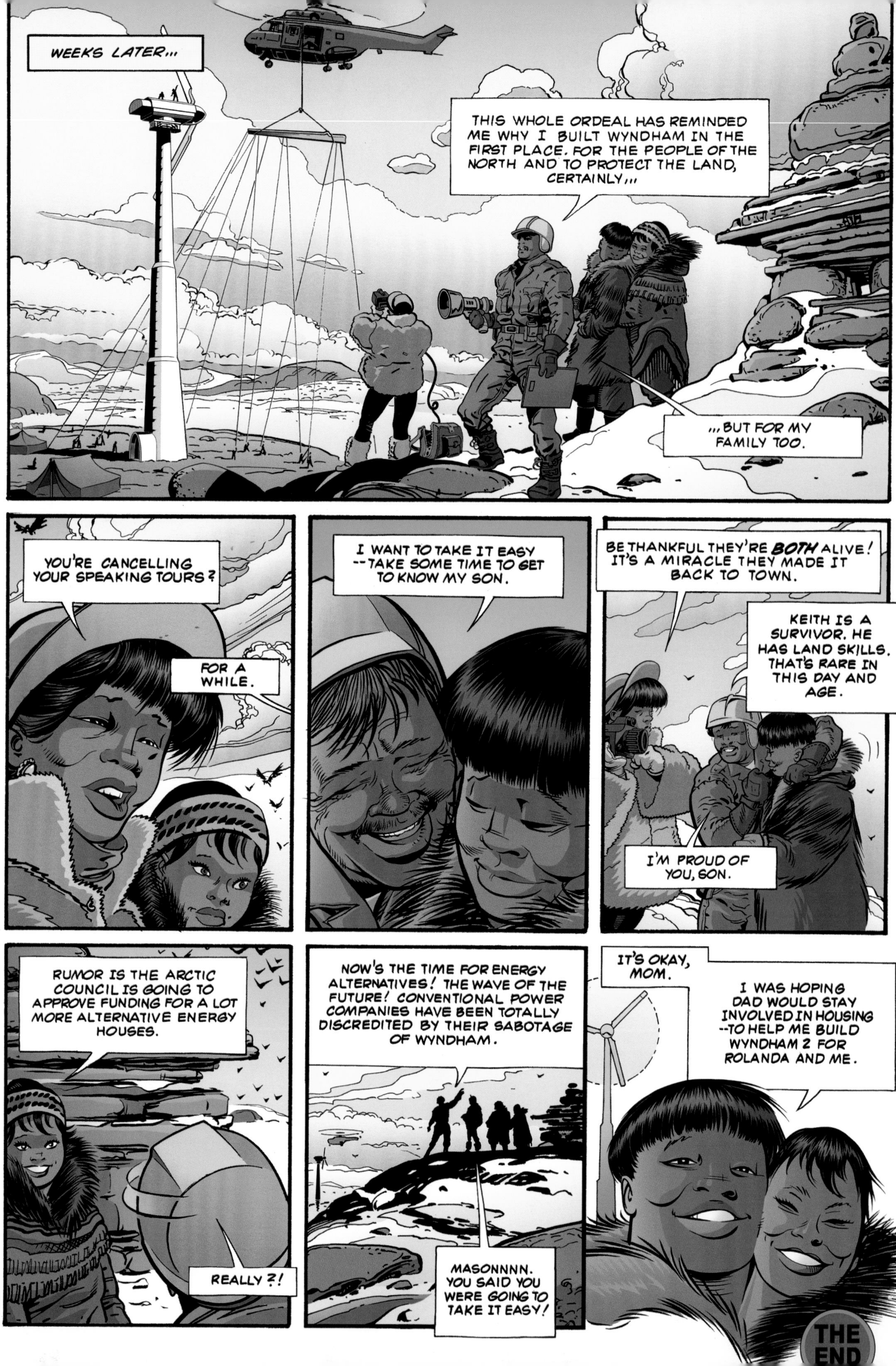
WEEKS LATER...
THIS WHOLE ORDEAL HAS REMINDED ME WHY I BUILT WYNDHAM IN THE FIRST PLACE. FOR THE PEOPLE OF THE NORTH AND TO PROTECT THE LAND, CERTAINLY...
...BUT FOR MY FAMILY TOO.
YOU'RE CANCELLING YOUR SPEAKING TOURS?
FOR A WHILE.
I WANT TO TAKE IT EASY --TAKE SOME TIME TO GET TO KNOW MY SON.
BE THANKFUL THEY'RE BOTH ALIVE! IT'S A MIRACLE THEY MADE IT BACK TO TOWN.
KEITH IS A SURVIVOR. HE HAS LAND SKILLS. THAT'S RARE IN THIS DAY AND AGE.
I'M PROUD OF YOU, SON.
RUMOR IS THE ARCTIC COUNCIL IS GOING TO APPROVE FUNDING FOR A LOT MORE ALTERNATIVE ENERGY HOUSES.
REALLY?!
NOW'S THE TIME FOR ENERGY ALTERNATIVES! THE WAVE OF THE FUTURE! CONVENTIONAL POWER COMPANIES HAVE BEEN TOTALLY DISCREDITED BY THEIR SABOTAGE OF WYNDHAM.
MASONNNN. YOU SAID YOU WERE GOING TO TAKE IT EASY!
IT'S OKAY, MOM.
I WAS HOPING DAD WOULD STAY INVOLVED IN HOUSING --TO HELP ME BUILD WYNDHAM 2 FOR ROLANDA AND ME.
THE END